KING ARTHUR'S CAMLAN

by
LAURENCE
MAIN

Published in Wales by
Meirion Publications

Contact:
Laurence Main
9, Mawddwy Cottages
Minllyn, Dinas Mawddwy
Machynlleth
SY20 9LW
Tel: (01650) 531354

Text and maps © Laurence Main 2006
Illustrations and book design © Sarah Enoch (née Hughes) 1986 & 2006
Celtic designs courtesy of Dover Publications
Poems by Lisa Parfitt and Patricia John

ISBN 1 - 871974 - 11 - 9

Printed by Cambrian Printers, Aberystwyth

CONTENTS

	page
Acknowledgements	4
A piece in the jigsaw?	5
Picture inspired by Maelgwn Gwynedd	37
Poem: 'Camlan' by Elisabeth Oakland	39
The Dream of Derfel	40
The Battle of Camlan Walk and more	78
Location Map	82
Poems by Patricia John	83
Gweddi'r Derwydd	84
The Universal Druid Prayer	84

ACKNOWLEDGEMENTS

Special thanks are due to 'Aussie Annie', Pat Caveille, Sarah and Alan Enoch, Gaenor Evans, Graham Griffiths, Betty Mungham-Harris, Emma Orbach, Arthur Pendragon, Rosetta Reinke, Dill and Pete Revell, Raymond Street, Hayley Turner (née Griffiths),George Wemyss and Helen Woodley. Remarkable generosity and toleration has been extended towards me by Rev. Jim McKnight and his fellow Roman Catholic priests.

Two notable characters did not live to see the publication of this book, although I am well aware of their presence in spirit. I trust that my modest effort may serve the memory of the most stalwart of friends, Lisa Parfitt and David Evans. We shall meet again.

This book is dedicated to the goddess *Rhiannon.*

About the author:

This is Laurence Main's fiftieth book. Others include:

'Walk Snowdonia and North Wales' (Bartholomew)
'Mid Wales and the Marches Walks' (OS/Jarrold)
'Walks in Mysterious Wales' (Sigma)
'Family Walks in Mid Wales' (Scarthin)
'The Old Straight Tracks of Wessex' (Thornhill)
'In the Footsteps of King Arthur' (Western Mail)
'A Meirionnydd Coast Walk' (Gwasg Carreg Gwalch)
'The Spirit Paths of Wales' (Cicerone)

FORTHCOMING: 'The Spirit Paths of Gwynedd' (Meirion Publications)
'The Dyfi Valley Way' (Meirion Publications)

Front cover photo (by the author): Maes y Camlan from Bryn Cleifion

Back cover photo (by the author): The memorial stone to King Arthur at Meirion Mill, Dinas Mawddwy

Ꙗ piece in the jigsaw?

he story of King Arthur has captured the imagination of people all over the world and throughout centuries. Its very obscurity generates fascination. Instead of a recorded monarch, Arthur is a hero from a lost golden age. Yet there was a real King Arthur............

Many brilliant authors have created his image to fit their theories. The variety of their conclusions reveals how easy it is to conjure prejudice out of ignorance. Yet there are some things that can be stated with respect for truth. This little book deals with Camlan, the final battle which left Arthur mortally wounded. The place can be identified, as can some of the characters, suggesting why the battle happened.

There is much more to Arthur, of course. Many aspects will be touched upon, even the archetypal, celestial Arthur whose pattern appears in the landscape, related to Arth the Bear. The flesh and blood Arthur encountered here, however, lived and breathed around AD 500. The Scottish Arthur of a century later was probably named after him. Our Arthur is the one named in such ancient Welsh texts as *Culhwch and Olwen*.

He belongs to that tantalisingly obscure period between the Roman withdrawal from Britain and the chronicles of the monkish scribes. We do have references to Arthur, but of aural origin and written down centuries after his death.

Some people worship words written on paper or parchment, whilst despising those held in the memories of bardic descendants of the Druids (who were famous for their memory). The contemporary account we do

5

have suffers from being written by a man said to have destroyed, in a vengeful rage, works commemorating Arthur. This man was Gildas, pupil of 'St' Illtyd, whose surviving book has blackened the name of Gwynedd's King Maelgwn down the ages.

The term 'historian' must be used lightly when referring to Gildas. When Sabine Baring-Gould and J. Fisher compiled their *'Lives of the British Saints'* they formed the conclusion that 'the remembrance of Gildas as a masterful and unscrupulous man lingered on' (cf their entry on St Oudoceus). Baring-Gould and Fisher also knew the *real* Arthur. In their entry on St Padarn, they conclude:

'Arthur is spoken of as a tyrant, and wholly without heroic qualities, showing that the Life was composed before Geoffrey of Monmouth had thrown a false glamour over this disreputable prince, who generally figures in the Legends of the Welsh Saints as an egregious bully, with nothing of the 'White Arthur' about him'.

By contrast, their same entry on St Padarn records:

'Maelgwn was struck by blindness. This unfortunate and much abused King.....'

Uncle Arthur came from Gwent

Maelgwn was also a historical character, recorded as King of Gwynedd and dying in 547. Now we have a date to fix to a character of known location, we can build more around Maelgwn. He ruled Gwynedd, and Mawddwy was just within its boundary, then as now. Mawddwy's patron saint is Tydecho, who built his mother church at Llanymawddwy in 518 (his bones still lie beneath its altar*)* and his chapel at Mallwyd in  520. St Tydecho was granted leave to erect his first church and given other privileges by King Maelgwn, who gained the throne of Gwynedd in 517. Whatever you think of Arthur, the identity of St Tydecho is not queried. It is important then to realise that St Tydecho was the nephew of King Arthur and that Uncle Arthur hailed from Gwent (Monmouthshire). As Baring-Gould and Fisher noted, Tydecho was the son of Ammwn Ddu (King Arthur's Black Knight?) son of Emyr Llydaw (Budic, ruler of Brittany) and Anna, elder sister of Arthur and daughter of Meurig (of Gwent). It is also recorded that Tydecho's fair sister Tegfedd resided with him. Tydecho's more famous elder brother was St Samson. Strangely, few Arthurian

6

investigators take note of this clear identification of Arthur. He was the uncle of St Tydecho, younger brother of Anna and from Gwent.

Mawddwy lays claim to a major association with Arthur and his death. There are also minor associations with the young Arthur. As a prince he was fostered just north of the Aran mountains with Sir Cai at Caergai, near Llanuwchllyn. When he grew his first beard he slew the giant Rhita on the slopes of Aran Benllyn and Rhita's grave is located near grid reference *SH 912 244 (*Tan y Bwlch). This was not Arthur's territory, which was in South-east Wales, Gloucestershire and Somerset. Arthur was the pendragon, or overall warlord, but the rulers of Gwynedd were descended from Cunedda, of whom Maelgwn was a great-grandson.

Strategic position
Dinas Mawddwy overlooks the ancient frontier between Gwynedd and Powys where the old Roman road from Viriconium (Wroxeter) used to ford the holy river that traditionally divided Wales, the Afon Dyfi (diving like a dove from the mountains to the sea). This road continued up Cwm Cerist and over Bwlch Oerddrws to reach Brithdir, where a Roman fortlet guarded its junction with the road from Chester. Check Ordnance Survey Explorer Map OL 23. Dinas Mawddwy is at *SH 858 147.* Sarn Helen passed nearby on its way from Carmarthen to Caerhun. Dinas Mawddwy is, therefore, a strategic place. Important battles occur at such spots.

One of the most important battles of the sixth century was fought at Camlan, as in Maes y Camlan *(SH 857 132)* and Camlan *(SH 821 169).* Just over four miles apart and connected, as this little book will reveal. Cwm Camlan *(SH 715 246)* on OS Explorer OL18 is where a skirmish took place in the same battle. *'The Welsh Triads'* (no. 84) describe it as the worst of the 'Three Futile Battles of the Island of Britain'. Camlan resulted in the death of King Arthur. Several writers have searched their maps for the Camlan name. They approach it bearing all sorts of conflicting theories. Their conclusions are the same regarding Arthur's last battle, however. It took place near Dinas Mawddwy.

Conflicting theories that don't hit the bull's eye
Philips and Keatman, for example, wrote ingenious fiction in their *'King Arthur - The True Story',* but at least they recognise

'that the only location in Great Britain ever to have been called Camlan is precisely and strategically in the border area of the kingdoms of Gwynedd and Powys as they existed in the early sixth century'.

7

I remember contacting Baram Blackett and Alan Wilson in the late 1980s to congratulate them upon recognising 'our' Camlan in their book *'Artorius Rex'*. In the early 1980s (before the publication of their book) I had been lent a copy of *'Dinas Mawddwy a'i Hamgylchoedd'* by Thomas Davies *(Tegwyn)* which had won an Eisteddfod prize in 1893. This was written in Welsh and mentioned the local tradition that Camlan was fought near Dinas Mawddwy.

The renowned Rodney Castleden hit the dartboard but not the bull's eye in his book *'King Arthur – the Truth Behind the Legend'*. He plumped for Cwm Camlan at *SH 715 246* (Ganllwyd) because there was 'no tradition to support' Camlan being fought in Mawddwy. But, Mr Castleden, there *is* a strong local tradition for Camlan in Mawddwy! In 1984 a local school-leaver asked me to employ her (I then worked for the Vegan Society, whose office occupied an old shop in Dinas Mawddwy). This girl showed me her local history project, which I have retained. Hayley Griffiths was her name and she came from an old local family, whose memories she was able to draw upon. Hayley wrote about Camlan, mentioning Nant Saeson *(SH 921 130)*, five miles east of the battlefield of Maes y Camlan *(SH 857 132)*, where Saxon mercenaries camped beside the Roman road from Viriconium the night before the battle. Hayley concluded:

'Mawddwy is not really considered as a possible site for the battle today, but the villagers will always believe one day someone might come to this area and who knows what they will find, but we believe and that's what matters.'

Rodney Castleden's lack of local research for his book on King Arthur is made obvious when he locates the Sword Stone at Sylfaen (*SH 633 186* on OS Explorer OL 18) and purports to show a picture of it! The real Sword Stone is marked Cerrig y Cledd on the map at *SH 643 199*, one mile away. I pity the American tourists using Rodney Castleden's book.

Christopher Gidlow is better in his book *'The Reign of Arthur'*. This contains a picture of 'Camlan on the Dyfi in North Wales'. This is taken from *SH 858 123*, south of the actual battlefield of Maes y Camlan, but close to it. Clustered near this viewpoint are the place names Camlan, Bron Camlan and Camlan Uchaf. Above is Bwlch Cae Tomen, the field with a burial mound for corpses for those who tried to go over the hill in an attempt to outflank their enemy. Most fighting took place at Maes y Camlan. On the eastern side of the river from this is Bryn Cleifion, translated as hillside of the wounded, where the wounded were laid to rest.

8

Evidence from place names

Place name evidence is strongly in favour of Camlan being fought where there is a bend in the river near Dinas Mawddwy. Maes y Camlan, the field where the battle started and finished, even has a tributary of the Afon Dyfi flowing through its southern corner. This is Nant y Gamell and is the very 'crooked stream' that some see at Camelford, despite the fact that Saxons and Cornish clashed there centuries *after* Arthur.

Local farmers tell me how relevant objects have been revealed by ploughing at Maes y Camlan. Bones were uncovered when the old railway station and the Buckley Arms Hotel (now the Buckley Pines Hotel) were constructed in the nineteenth century. It is reasonable, therefore, to propose that Camlan *really was* fought near Dinas Mawddwy. The date given for this is 537, although some scribes have written 539 or 542. 537 feels better to me and would allow Maelgwn Gwynedd a further ten years to reign before his own death, recorded as being in 547. The battle was both spread over several days and fought on a Thursday. This suggests skirmishes on days building up to the main event, followed by mopping-up exercises. Harleian manuscript 4181 entry 42 names Arthur's assailant as Eda Elyn Mawr, son of Gwynber Dorchog son of Mug Mawr Drefydd, son of Alla Gyllell Fawr.

Battle survivors

In the Mabinogion tale of *'Culhwch and Olwen'* there is a specific reference to three survivors of the last battle. They were

'Morfran, son of Tegid (no man placed his weapon in him at Camlan, so exceedingly ugly was he; all thought he was a devil helping. There was hair on him like the hair on a stag), and Sandde Angel-face (no one placed his spear in him at Camlan, so exceedingly fair was he; all thought he was an angel helping), and Cynwyl the Saint (one of the three men that escaped from Camlan. He was the last to part from Arthur, on Hengroen his horse)'.

So, we even know the name of Arthur's horse, Hengroen or 'Old Skin'. This St Cynwyl was a brother of the St Deiniol who became the first Bishop of Bangor during the reign of Maelgwn Gwynedd. Cynwyl went on to found the church at Aberporth in Ceredigion, still under the overlordship of Maelgwn, so his presence at Camlan would support a site on the border of Gwynedd. Tegid lived at Bala and his son, Morfran, may be the same person as or a brother to the Afagddu of the Taliesin legend. He was the son of Ceridwen, wife of Tegid. Elphin occurs in the same story. Both Taliesin and Elphin are recorded in association with Maelgwn Gwynedd and also with the estuary of the Afon Dyfi, on the border of Gwynedd.

Supernatural stirrings, secrets being revealed
The supernatural is ever present in the Arthurian tale and it was an ever present reality to the historical characters in it. At this point I would briefly mention an interesting and perceptive book by a visionary artist and friend of mine. It is *'Behold Jerusalem!'* by Graham Griffiths. This is about a great landscape zodiac. It came into my life after I had prayed on Beltaine Eve at the stone circle formed by the daughters of Long Meg, in Cumbria, whilst walking a 1,404 mile pilgrimage through Britain to celebrate the Diamond Jubilee of the Vegan Society in 2004. I asked for the secrets contained in the landscape of the Cross Fell area to be revealed to me. Within a fortnight there they were when Graham Griffiths' book came into my hands. I knew his book made sense because it also showed Dinas Mawddwy as nestling in the womb of the goddess (the Virgo figure in the zodiac). I had been writing and telling people this for over a decade, so knew we had both divined the same truth.

This goddess is the Ceridwen who gave birth to Taliesin at the mouth of the Dyfi. Cynics may delight in disparaging something they cannot understand. This lack of understanding, of spiritual appreciation, is the great failing of our time. Hence, for now, note it briefly and simply accept that the presence of a Morfrân son of Tegid at Camlan does strengthen the claim for the Dinas Mawddwy site. Dafydd Nanmor wrote:

'In Camlan of the British there were unslain from the two sides seven men, who went from the field. One is by his spear a saint. Pedrog was famous with his steel, precious, at the time of Arthur's death'.

The 'Magnificent Seven'
The seven survivors were the aforementioned Sandde Angel-face, linked to Meirionnydd and local to a battle near Dinas Mawddwy, plus Morfran son of Tegid (also local), then comes St Cynfelin from the speed of his horse (who gave his name to Sarn Cynfelin near Borth, another local connection), St Cedwyn from *'the world's blessing'* (linked to Montgomeryshire, so another local), St Pedrog from the strength of his spear (Pedrog's spear was exhibited in his church at Llanbedrog, Gwynedd in 1535, according to Sir Lewis Newburgh. Pedrog also has a church at Y Ferwig, near Cardigan),

10

Derfel Gadarn (the Strong) from his strength and Geneid the Tall from his speed. Relevantly, Derfel Gadarn has a local connection in that he later became a saint and founded the church at Llandderfel, near Bala. *He has much more to contribute later in this book............*

I know nothing more about Geneid the Tall. It is obvious that the survivors would fit the site of the battle as being near Dinas Mawddwy. *Being able to make such a definite statement is a rare thing for Arthurian times.* This is one piece of the jigsaw that can be surely placed, whatever theories speculation builds.

Why here?
As an avid reader of 'Pendragon', the journal of the Pendragon Society (contact Simon and Anne Rouse, 7 Verlon Close, Montgomery, Powys, SY15 6SH), I enjoy the many and varied theories put forward by members regarding the life, times and death of King Arthur. Without realising it until later, I have been drawn to various Arthurian locations. I do enjoy enlivening my walking routes with references to Arthurian connections. What follows is a result of dreams and happenings. I promised a friend (whom I never met in this life) that it would appear. A novelist would write a novel. I write guidebooks. Quite simply, I am obliged to record the truth – *'Y Gwir yn Erbyn y Byd'* (The Truth against the World).

Saints, satanists and wizards
Beginning as conventionally as possible, we know that one survivor of Camlan was Derfel Gadarn. It might pay to investigate this character, explaining his presence at the battle. Elissa Henken has collected a few references to him in her book *'Traditions of the Welsh Saints'*, including

'Derfel in war would work his spear wondrously, steel covering is the garment, brave is the appearance'.

His connection with Gwynedd is made clear with:

'By Derfel the land of Arfon was gotten'.

Derfel's presence at Camlan is emphasised:

'when there was at Camlan men and fighting and a host being slain, Derfel with his arms was dividing steel there in two'.

Derfel is recorded as the son of Hywel, son of Emyr Llydaw. Hywel was one of the 'Three Royal Knights of Arthur's Court', whilst Emyr Llydaw was the ruler of Brittany. Derfel was, indeed, born in Brittany (near Brest). His

11

later link to Gwynedd would demand an explanation. He became a saint and his image was kept in the church at Llandderfel, Meirionnydd. He ended his days as the (third) Abbot of Ynys Enlli (Bardsey Island). Referring to Derfel in *'The Matter of Wales'*, Jan Morris wrote:

'The reputation of this ambiguous anchorite was dark but compelling……..Some believed him to be one of Arthur's knights, withdrawn from the world of chivalry, while many thought him more a wizard than a saint, and linked his name with Satanic cults'.

Translate *'Satanic'* into *'Goddess'* and remember the power of such propaganda lay with the patriarchal Church of Rome, that antithesis of the Way of Jesus.

Read John Cowper Powys' 'Owen Glendower' for the juicy bits about his reputation with the ladies (and as a warrior) even in the later Middle Ages:

'Her were a dedicated nun; and to bear a baban for Derfel were too much for the maid'.

'Saint Derfel! Saint Derfel! they cried as they brandished their spears'.

'The bare-legged Derfel-worshippers had now lighted a bonfire of their own'.

'Thus the Latin of the monks and the Welsh of Derfel's prophet answered each other across that misty expanse'.

'You English don't understand these things; but in these parts Derfel's held to be more than a saint'.

'….girls like me at any rate, are always being warned by the priests to have nothing to do with these Derfel men'.

'He always knows when a girl's in love because his Horse begins neighing when he rides around the house'.

'When the wind's in the west and rain's coming that he rides; and when a girl hears Derfel's Horse she knows she's found out'.

'In those old times,' he went on while his followers' eyes flashed in sympathy, 'there were <u>real</u> saints among us! Saint Derfel, Saint Tisilio, Saint Collen – wouldn't any of <u>them</u> as soon fling a spear at a Gwyddel from Ireland, or Silurian from Gwent, as at any serf-Saxon or bastard-Norman!'

'…..if Wales is ever liberated it will be through hot-heads and madmen, through bards and Derfelites…….'

12

'There's Derfel making his moan – he's asking for a new maidenhead!'

'Saint Derfel' – *and the Friar crossed himself devoutly* – *'is in the company of the Blest; but there are those in the heathen places of this land, who conjure up terrible evil in the blessed one's name!'*

'I suppose you lads have never heard of Saint Derfel and his Horse? Well, for many hundreds of years this curious Being has been the object of what to my mind is undoubtedly a most interesting heathen cult. The Church of our ancestors, as I always say, were wise in assuming the canonisation of this queer figure, though I doubt myself whether the Holy Father had anything to do with it!'

'They say that the people of Ardudwy will rise in greater numbers if Derfel has a new bride'.

'....the daughter of Rhys ap Tudor had resolved to be Derfel's bride!'

'The men'll cry 'Derfel' tomorrow', he announced bluntly, 'whatever we decide for them!'

'Derfel Gadarn, our Patron and Protector'.

'But what I don't think any of them counted on was Derfel's horse'.

'Derfel's rod being like an axle-tree.....'

I have no idea how John Cowper Powys came to conjure up the above quotations, but he did. Hardly a relevant historical source, but they ring true to me. George Borrow in his *'Wild Wales'* was taken with the character of Derfel Gadarn too.

'....Pray what is the meaning of Darfel Gatherel ?',

'O sir!' said the landlord, 'you must answer that question yourself; I don't pretend to understand gibberish!'

Here beginneth the gibberish............

Simply wishing to record the truth, I wrote magazine articles about King Arthur's Camlan having been fought at Dinas Mawddwy, as Hayley Griffiths had written in her school local history project. The essence of these was conveyed in my booklet *'Arthur's Camlan'*. This described walks in the area and was published in 1989. It also tried to paint a picture of the Arthurian scene, suggesting why Camlan was fought here. I was not being inspired. Instead I tried to make the theories of others fit the one fact I did know. I therefore ventured to suggest that Maelgwn Gwynedd was Sir Lancelot. That comment was to return to me (see below). Knowing what I do in 2006, I must emphasise that Maelgwn was *not* Sir Lancelot! Neither was he the other bad things that Illtyd's protégés alleged.

By the way, I'm sure that King Arthur's neighbour Gwynlliw was Sir Lancelot. In a curious way Gwynlliw may even have been Arthur's superior in Gwent, so he was a true *l'ancelot* in the French sense of being one who actually serves an inferior. Arthur was king in the sense of being overall warlord of all the British kingdoms against the Saxon invaders. Gwynlliw was a notorious womaniser, his wife St Gwladus would have nothing to do with him, Arthur was away and Gwenhwyfar was handy. Gwynlliw was also the father of Catwg and Sabine Baring-Gould and Fisher reckon St Catwg (or Cadoc) was Sir Galahad. Sir Galahad was the son of Sir Lancelot. Seems simple to me!

On with the gibberish.............
From 1993 my mind was turned to the dreaming project on Carn Ingli, the sacred peak in Pembrokeshire. I have written a bit about this in my book *'The Spirit Paths of Wales'* (Cicerone Press). A dream in 1993 revealed a date to me. On that day in June 1994, the lady I now know to have been Derfel's Rhiannon (see *'The Dream of Derfel'*) came to my tent. The day before I'd had the television cameras and a man who believes himself to be the reincarnation of King Arthur dreaming with me. Arthur had contacted me 'out of the blue' (we didn't know each other) just when S4C TV wanted to film a dreamer on Carn Ingli.

Visions of a stone
Returning from that trip to Carn Ingli, I was informed by Mr Raymond Street of Meirion Mill that whilst I'd been away, he'd had a dream and already acted upon it. His vision was of a memorial stone to King Arthur on his land next to Maes y Camlan, the battlefield. I had nothing to do with this. If I had, I would have dowsed for where leys cross, being the appropriate place for such a stone. I did suggest to Mr Street that the reincarnation of King Arthur might unveil it. So he did, on 4th July 1994. That date was best for the local school, who fully participated in the ceremony. Years later I realised that if you add 11 days for the change in the calendar, this was 23rd June in the days of King Arthur. Dreams (see below) showed the battle as being fought on Maes y Camlan a couple of days after the Summer Solstice, 21st June 537. By coincidence, we had unveiled the stone on the anniversary of the battle.

> *'There is nothing in that which men say, to wit, that a thing happens by chance.'*
> King Alfred the Great

14

The unveiling ceremony included the blessing of the stone by Dylan ap Thuin, an archdruid used to working with Arthur at Stonehenge. Dylan arrived at the last minute, as the children were forming the procession. Donning his robes, he followed me as I went well in advance of everybody to the stone, intending to meet the procession there. As I approached the stone, I found myself doing and saying things over which I had no control, as if in a dizzy whirl. I remember seeing a stone the size of my hand at my feet, like a chip off the memorial stone. Picking it up, I found myself hammering the top of the memorial stone with it and saying words in rhyme and to the effect that this stone was to cleanse the battlefield, to release the energies and to connect it with the network of leys. I sent its spirit to the local parish church, St Tydecho's at Mallwyd. I shall never

know if the stone marked a ley before the ceremony, or even before its erection. I didn't dowse for a ley until afterwards. There is a ley there now, connecting the stone with the altar of the church at Mallwyd.

The stone was unveiled by the reincarnation of the man it commemorated with due ceremony and a poem emphasising reconciliation, written as I returned by bus from Carn Ingli that 24th June (the very anniversary, as I later realised, of King Arthur's death).

> On Camlan's field a stone we raise,
> That it may wield our note of praise
> And lay to rest the adder's work,
> With all the woe that strife imparts.
> Time has healed the wounds of Arthur,
> Forgiven Medrawt for the slaughter.
> Together now, with one accord,
> We acknowledge Arthur as our lord.
> Truth, honour, justice, must once again
> Ride triumphant in his reign.

15

Bard dreams and a knighthood on Carn Ingli

What would you do if you received a letter from the re-incarnation of King Arthur asking you if you would agree to be raised up as a knight and, if so, what would your name be? I agreed and said that I thought it was important to live this life now, rather than to seek previous lives, so I wished to become Sir Laurence. Arthur wanted to dream on Carn Ingli again, so he said he would knight me there at Hallowe'en (1994). A garbled account of this fills the early pages of *'The Trials of Arthur'* by Arthur Pendragon and C.J.Stone. Here is the more accurate version. Expecting him to arrive alone on his motorcycle by 2 pm, I was afraid the ceremony would not take place when, just before dusk on the darkest night of that month, King Arthur appeared in a car driven by a friend, Taliesin. He had been in a crash in Cardiff a couple of days before, broken his left arm and badly bruised his thighs. Discharging himself from hospital, he had persuaded Taliesin to hire a car and drive him.

At the top of the hill in the dark, he turned to me and said his bard, Taliesin, was here, his Myrddin Wyllt (Merlin), meaning me in the guise of the wild man of the mountain, was here, as was the King himself. All he needed now was a virgin! I turned and said, 'Arthur, I can't find you a virgin.' 'Don't worry,' he said, 'one will come.'

There are moments when you doubt your sanity and those around you. And then you are left bemused by the rapid course of events. Looking through the darkness to the foot of the hill, I notice a tiny sliver of light. A local woman (Old Derfel's Rhiannon, first met that June) who knew King Arthur was up Carn Ingli with me that night had given a lift to a nineteen year-old girl straight out of a convent in Nova Scotia who was heading for the Irish ferry at Fishguard. This lady had persuaded her to delay crossing the Irish Sea in order to meet King Arthur on top of Carn Ingli. This she did.

When King Arthur raised me up as a knight he did so in my present name but added 'in the spirit of Sir Derfel'. *I had to pick up my old Quest.*

False priests

All of us on the sacred peak that night shared a common dream in which false priests, hooded and bearing crosses came through a trap-door in the Underworld. There was a mighty battle in which King Arthur defended the maiden from their advances. My role in the dream was to shut the gates of the city, then defend its battlements. It seemed to me that this was like the siege of Derry, the 'Maiden City'. When its Protestant defenders were at

military history), their spirits were revived by a vision in the night sky of a white horse. Then it struck me. The goddess of Carn Ingli is Rhiannon, of the white horse. Rhiannon was on the side of the defenders of Derry (against the patriarchal priests of Rome). The siege of Derry started when thirteen brave Apprentice Boys shut the gates in the face of King James II. Thirteen refers to the lunar months in a year and indicates the Goddess. Ulster mythology always has King William of Orange riding a white horse, yet it is a known historical fact that he rode a dun coloured horse. The symbolic horse must be white.

We seem to have strayed a long way from Camlan, but there is one more obscure detail:

'Then here's to the boys who fear no noise,
Who never will surrender!
The gates we closed against our foes
On the 18th of December.'

So sing the Apprentice Boys of Derry. The 18th of December also happens to be one of the two festivals of the goddess Rhiannon. The other, 11th November, is the old date for Hallowe'en and the goddess Rhiannon's Initiation Day, or Night. I was unaware of this when I spent that very night in 1994 on Carn Ingli with the lady I know to have been Derfel's Rhiannon (see later, *The Dream of Derfel*). It was an Initiation Night. See below also for the story of Tegfedd. The 18th of December is also the festival of St Tegfedd.

17

Hey, it's King Arthur on the phone!

I didn't hear from King Arthur again until the next August, 1995. The reincarnation of Sir Bedwyr had called with some friends to see the stone at Camlan. I conducted them to it and we held hands around it and sent out best wishes to our king. That night *(coincidence!)* Arthur telephoned me for the first time since raising me up as a knight the previous Hallowe'en. He wished to know if his memorial stone was alright because it had been on his mind all day.

Ill-tidings and heresy

July and August of 1995 saw new developments in the dreaming on Carn Ingli. An English lady that July had to spell out M-A-E-L-G-W-N because she saw it in a dream and didn't know what it meant. Another was greeted by Pan or Cernunnos in Tycanol Wood, below Carn Ingli, before adding to a group of dreamers seeing the figure of a sinister, hooded monk in their dreams around Lugnasadh. The previous year had featured the cheerful, friendly, St Brynach. The name that came through now was Illtyd. This episode culminated with a powerful night under a full moon that 6th November – St Illtyd's Day. *Old 'Ill-tide'*, as I came to call him, was a cousin of King Arthur who studied in Paris and became a disciple of St Germanus of Auxerre, who was sent by the Pope of Rome to suppress the Pelagian heresy in Britain in the fifth century. Pelagius may have been an Ulsterman who believed in reincarnation and the law of cause and effect, rather than original sin. After serving as a soldier, Illtyd separated from his wife (he was a misogynist and, as later dreams revealed, a paederast) and became a monk. He loved to control through fear in an institutional setting designed to crush the spirit. He established a college at what is now called Llantwit Major (Llanilltyd Fawr). Here he educated, or indoctrinated, the sons of the nobility, including Gildas, Samson, Tydecho, Taliesin, Maelgwn and Derfel.

Maelgwn Gwynedd and strange meetings

August, 1995, was also when a man from Birmingham telephoned me for the first time. His name in this life was David Evans and he was housebound, suffering from epilepsy and kidney disease. He was also very psychic, being able to 'go out' from his body at will (proving this in astounding ways) and was the reincarnation of Maelgwn Gwynedd. David's sister had treated him to a drive in her car to Wales. David knew to ask her to come to Dinas Mawddwy. He was surprised to buy there, at

Meirion Mill, my booklet on *'Arthur's Camlan'*. He was well aware at this stage that he was the reincarnation of Maelgwn Gwynedd and was expecting soon to team up with his old friend Derfel Gadarn. *Not that he told me any of this when he first contacted me.*

David's method was always to provoke questions and to point the way for you to stumble upon the answer yourself, which he would then substantiate. He wanted to know why I thought Maelgwn Gwynedd might be Sir Lancelot. He encouraged me to dig further for the truth and then to write about it. The *real* story of Camlan needed to be told. Hence this book. I already knew by now that I was the reincarnation of Derfel Gadarn but took the attitude that the past was the past and that it's this life that matters now. Quests, of course, span several lifetimes. The story of Derfel came out in bits and pieces through dreams, strange meetings and happenings over subsequent years. I haven't sought it. It is subjective. As history, it counts for nought. It is highly relevant to Camlan, however. It is a unique insight. I also promised David that I would set the record straight. It inspired my ballad *'The Dream of Derfel'* (see later).

Far from having the whole picture, tiny segments have been revealed to me. One of the best books on King Arthur is *'Journey to Avalon'* by David Pykitt and my friend Chris Barber (who witnessed the unveiling of the memorial stone on 4th July, 1994). It pains me to disagree with him on the matter of Camlan's location (and the death of Arthur, whom Chris Barber sees living on in Brittany as St Armel, who was actually Derfel's brother).

Medrawt features little in my story. Maelgwn/David told me that Medrawt would never be allowed to accede to Arthur's throne (indeed, I think Cuneglasus finished him off at Camlan). *That whole affair was a device used by Illtyd to send his puppet King Arthur north to destroy Maelgwn.*

Dreamy recollections and historical evidence

My earliest recollection of Derfel (from the dreams), however, is of him suckling at one breast as Medrawt did the same at the other. The mother was Medrawt's, not Derfel's, being Gwyar, elder sister of King Arthur (and Anna, mother of St Tydecho, with whom she has been confused by some scribes). I also knew that Gwyar was, in some strange way, superior to Derfel's mother (Pompeia) despite Pompeia being older than her. Years later, I happened upon Rachel Bromwich's notes to personal names in her translation of *'The Welsh Triads' (Trioedd Ynys Prydain).* Checking Gwalchmai m. Gwyar I read (from the fourteenth century *'Birth Of Arthur'*),

'Gwyar was (living as) a widow in her father's court, and Hywel her son with her, after the death of Ymer Llydaw her husband. And Uthyr caused Lleu ap Cynfarch to marry her, and they had children: that is two sons Gwalchmai and Medrawd, and three daughters, Gracia, Graeria and Dioneta'.

Sense can be made of this when my dream is taken into account. Gwyar was about twenty years of age. I agree with Chris Barber that Arthur was born in 482 and would have been sixteen in 498, when Derfel was born. Gwyar was older than Arthur and had seduced him, becoming pregnant with Medrawt. She was married off to Budic, ruler of Brittany (Emyr Llydaw), to be out of the way and to satisfy old Budic's desires. Thus, young Gwyar really did become the *step*-mother of Hywel (who was about a dozen years older than Arthur) and the *step*-grandmother of Derfel.

Budic soon died, so Gwyar returned to the court of Meurig (who bore the title of Uther and was Arthur's father) where her 'son' Hywel was an important counsellor and military advisor to Arthur, before marrying Lleu and bearing him Gwalchmai (Gawain). I would never have spotted this obscure reference if I hadn't realised here was a scrap of historical evidence for what my dream showed me.

Riding to freedom

Derfel rescued Maelgwn from Illtyd's advances at that dreadful school. David Evans woke up one night with such a powerful dream that he had to telephone me immediately. It was one of headmaster Illtyd assaulting pupil Maelgwn but being accidentally interrupted by Derfel. That very morning, turning on the radio, the news was of one of the pope's top officials being found dead *(the same night as the dream)* in his boyfriend's flat in Rome. There have been many revelations of clerical abuse since that dream. I then dreamt of riding to freedom with Maelgwn sharing my horse, in classical Templar mode.

20

Hywel, Derfel's father, took his family to Pembrokeshire, where his church stands in Llanhowel (*SM 819 275* on Explorer OL 35). Llanrhian is nearby in what was the land of the Demetii. Derfel's first campaign was in what is now Anjou, France, then the home of the Andecavi. King Arthur knighted young Derfel in Lichfield. He fought in Arthur's battles and patrolled part of his border whilst based at what became interestingly named Kingston Deverill, then he helped Maelgwn gain the throne of Gwynedd in 517 and he stayed there.

Itchy feet at the start of the Quest
One of the first people to meet me at the start of my Quest was Pat from St Neot's. We meet annually and there is always a happy, playful, childish relationship. Pat dreamt of us running hand in hand along a beach as children, with I the elder. In June, 2001, I happened to lead Pat on a walk along part of my *'Meirionnydd Coast Walk'* (Gwasg Carreg Gwalch) and we paused at a spring called Ffynnon Enddwyn (*SH 613 255* On OS Explorer OL 18). I knew nothing about this spring apart from its name and my guidebook, written in 2000, reflected that fact (cf its page 80). There was a new information board beside it giving the story of Enddwyn healing her infected feet with its moss. Pat had almost not come on that walk. She arrived in Wales with a fungal infection on her feet. Pat washed her feet as Enddwyn had in the sacred spring and stuffed moss around them when we left (her feet did heal). We intended to climb a mountain the next day. Dawn came and there was heavy rain, so we went for a drive. Puzzled by St Enddwyn, we ended up at her church near Dyffryn Ardudwy railway station. I'd never been in it before. It's normally shut but we happened to meet the lady vicar just as she was locking up. Because of this fortunate coincidence, the vicar was able to proudly show us her church's new icon of St Enddwyn, freshly painted and delivered. Later I went to Dolgellau Library to see what Sabine Baring-Gould and J. Fisher had to say about St Enddwyn. Enddwyn was a daughter of Hywel and a sister of Derfel Gadarn. Like her brother she ended up in Gwynedd. Is Pat the reincarnation of Enddwyn? I say so. Only the two of us can really intuit the truth of that. *We did not seek this chance happening.*

The lone ranger and the exotic dancer
Derfel guarded Maelgwn's borders and went on campaigns with Gwynedd's allies, notably Dal Riada. My Quest has led me to sites on the Isle of Man, in Northern Ireland and in Scotland (including the Ayrshire town of Darvel with its interesting stone). Govan (named after Gawain) is a favourite part of Glasgow. Maelgwn gave him a palace near Ffestiniog (Llys Dorfil at *SH*

696 444 on OS Explorer OL18) but Derfel was happier in a hut overlooking Ynys Lawd on Ynys Gybi (*SH 212 820* on OS Explorer 262).

Dreaming in what I knew to be the circle of 'my hut' above Ynys Lawd in July, 1999, I first encountered the feel of 'my family'. I couldn't be sure if there were five or six children. I knew by now their mother couldn't be Rhiannon yet couldn't understand how Derfel could be married to anyone else. In March, 2001, David Evans came through with vivid dreams involving a party at Deganwy, an exotic dancer and Derfel raising a family with her above Ynys Lawd. We still couldn't be sure if there were five or six children (my dowsing suggested both) and wondered what happened to them since they suddenly disappeared. I had a dream of a most  beautiful tanned woman with a very slim waist, long dark curly hair and knew she came from the east. The message was she was back here in this life, in the east. I thought she might be a Pakistani living in, say, Leicester. I performed a summoning ritual, choosing to do so on 5th April, 2001, because that was St Derfel's Day. Nothing happened, so I repeated this summoning ritual on 17th April, 2001, because that is my birthday in this life.

Australian dream-time
Normally I'd be on the sacred peak of Carn Ingli for my birthday but couldn't because of the Foot and Mouth Disease restrictions. I imagined I was there. On Wednesday, 6th June, 2001, I visited Uffington white horse (the emblem of the goddess Rhiannon) with Helen from Bath (Aquae Sulis) and saw a kestrel as I prayed in the eye of the white horse. That was a good sign and on Thursday evening, 7th June, 2001, I returned home to a telephone call from M. (whose story appears later, being the Spirit of Deganwy). M. knew I had summoned my exotic dancer from the east because she had turned up with my birthday present as I was performing the summoning ceremony that 17th April. She felt sure she had met the lady. M. happened to call on the warden at Corris Youth Hostel and met his new assistant, a lady on a working holiday from Australia. Her name was Annie and she was told nothing about my dream or Quest. We soon arranged to meet for a walk with M. that Saturday, 9th June, 2001. Aussie Annie was the lady of my dream. I recognised her instantly. I told her nothing. Annie told me how she'd realised in July, 1999 (when I first dreamt in 'our' hut) that she must make her first trip out of Australia, to

Wales. Of Welsh blood, she was extremely psychic and felt drawn to the Ynys Lawd area.

Life-changing events had occurred to Annie in the summer of 1999, as had been the case with me. She had decided to sell her vineyard in Queensland (about as far east as you could be from Wales) and make the trip. The day she landed at Heathrow was 5th April, 2001 *(when I first summoned her on St Derfel's Day)*. She headed for Wales and unusually for a tourist she stayed in youth hostels in the hope of finding work as an assistant warden.

She was in Newport (Trefdraeth) in Pembrokeshire on my birthday, 17th *April, 2001 (when I summoned her again)*. Learning about the sacred peak of Carn Ingli, overlooking Newport, she wished to climb it but couldn't because of Foot and Mouth restrictions (as I couldn't). So she bought a book in the bookshop. It was *'The Spirit Paths of Wales'* by Laurence Main (Cicerone Press).

I must re-emphasise that neither I nor M. told her anything about my dream or Quest. Annie unfolded the public transport map of Wales and showed me where she wanted to go next, through Ynys Môn (Isle Of Anglesey) to the bus terminus at South Stack. She knew that had to be her destination, the reason for her trip. I had met her intending to ask her to travel to that very terminus with me, then dream in (I didn't tell her 'our') this pre-historic hut circle nearby. Aussie Annie readily agreed. On the bus going there I gave her a sealed envelope containing the story of the dreams of David Evans and myself. I told her not to open it until the morning. That night, Annie squeezed my hand and said she knew this place, it had been her home. She also knew me, I'd been her husband, no, not her husband but

23

as if I were her husband. We'd been happy together and had five children with a *sixth* on the way. Annie dreamt of being a dancer in a smoke-filled hall (at Deganwy) and then becoming my concubine because it wasn't done for princes to marry captured dancers.

Princesses and priestesses

Annie was a princess herself, however, from Thrace. A priestess, she had been sold into slavery as a result of war and came to Gwynedd on a boat with wine from Constantinople. Maelgwn had spent lavishly on a party for his friend Derfel's twenty-first birthday and to celebrate the birth of his first child (Princess Eurgain – Spirit of Deganwy – M.,).

Derfel was away campaigning with Dal Riada when raiders from southern Ireland attacked our hut and killed Annie and all our children. When Annie opened my sealed envelope in the morning, she had accounted for everything in it, settled the number of our children (being pregnant with the *sixth*) and added the news of how she and they were killed. Annie had known about Derfel's Rhiannon and knew that unlike in the old days, Rhiannon was still alive in this life for Derfel.

Summoning and awakening

David Evans first taught me to 'summon' in 1996, when I asked to be reunited with the reincarnation of Tegfedd (St Tydecho's sister and niece of King Arthur), as I recounted in my 1997 booklet *'Camlan – The True Story?'*. This booklet is now out of print, so I'll repeat the tale here. David Evans/Maelgwn telephoned me in the spring of 1996. He had a psychic message for me involving Ordnance Survey Explorer map OL 23. In Birmingham, his hand moved to the grid reference *SH 895 217* (approximately) on his map. This meant nothing to him. I knew it was where St Tydecho slept on the rocks and communed with the angels near Ffynnon Dydecho. I had been there with Richie Davies, the National Park warden, just a couple of months before, whilst walking the Dyfi Valley Way. I was told to go there on Beltaine Eve (30th April), spend the night there and 'awaken the sleepers', who were helmeted warriors in the rocks overlooking this spot. I went at the required time and, using my compass, marked the four cardinal points around my tent with stones brought from Carn Ingli. These made a circle of protection as I raised my arms at each point and said out loud, 'Sleepers, protect me'. I made a fire with rowan, apple and oak sticks brought from the shadow of Carn Ingli, plus an acorn. I invoked Maelgwn and the Dancer of the Dawn, then linked with Arthur and the sleepers. At dawn on May Day I visualised Dark Age warriors in grey, with face masks, chain mail, swords or lances and shields. I listened for

24

horse's hooves and meditated. It was my intention to continue that day to Carn Ingli. I just wanted to be on the sacred peak at Beltaine and to maintain the link which I had there. George, one of the people who dreamt regularly with me on Carn Ingli, was giving me a lift in his car. I walked down to Llanymawddwy to telephone George from the call box and settled down to wait in St Tydecho's church for about an hour till George would arrive at 9 am.

Beltaine journeys

Whilst waiting, I read again the old legend about St Tydecho and Maelgwn at Llanymawddwy. A copy can be seen at the back of the church. I have repeated it in my other guidebooks. This time, however, I noticed as if for the first time that it hadn't been just St Tydecho who had slept where I had awakened the sleepers. St Dogmael and St Tegfedd had lived there too. I knew Tegfedd was Tydecho's young sister, while Dogmael was a relative known for his honesty.

George arrived and drove me to Carn Ingli. It was too wet to stay the night (George's knee was aching), so we turned back towards Machynlleth. Wishing to make the most of the trip, we decided to visit somewhere on the way back. But where? I'd already shown George Pentre Ifan, the bleeding yew tree and the church at Nevern, Gors Fawr stone circle and Cerrig Meibion Arthur on earlier trips. Then I thought of St Dogmael's Abbey, where we saw the ogham stone and bought bread from the working watermill.

Tydecho's bed.....

Only as we drove further north did I realise that we had linked Tydecho's bed not only with Carn Ingli that Beltaine but with the abbey on the site of the place where all three saints, Tydecho, Dogmael, and Tegfedd, had lived for a while before coming to Llanymawddwy. What's more, I had read

25

in Llanymawddwy church that morning how Llanymawddwy was once called Llandudoch, just like St Dogmael's is today in Welsh, because of the connection between these two places. I hadn't known of that link or even of St Dogmael being in Mawddwy until that morning. We only chanced upon St Dogmael's because it had rained and George didn't feel up to a night in a tent. It seemed we had done the right thing.

.....and Derfel's chapel

Two weeks later I was in Cardiff making the final checks of my book on the Dyfi Valley Way being published by the Western Mail, for whom I also wrote weekly walks for the newspaper. I decided to break my journey on the way back, on Saturday, 18th May at Cwmbran. I would spend a few hours on a walk which I would write up for the Western Mail. My attention had been drawn to Cwmbran because I had been sent details of a pilgrimage starting there, at Llantarnam Abbey, on Thursday, 23rd May, 1996. I was intrigued by the fact that this went past a Capel Derfel. The organisers of the pilgrimage sent me details of this ruined chapel, confirming that it is associated with the sixth century St Derfel. I knew I wouldn't be able to go on the pilgrimage as I had dreamers coming from Yorkshire to Carn Ingli on Thursday, 23rd May, so I meant to walk to Capel Derfel and investigate Cwmbran's link with my previous incarnation.

Surprisingly, when I alighted from the train I decided all the new houses west of the station would spoil my walking route. Far more sensible was the option of walking east straight into the countryside along paths that had been waymarked and furnished with stiles, gates and signposts by the local Ramblers. I had a leaflet detailing a waymarked route, so I followed it and came to Llantegfedd, where there is the only church in the world dedicated to St Tegfedd. Was this the Tegfedd who had lived near Llanymawddwy with her brother Tydecho? The church was locked and I didn't go for the key as I was afraid of being late for my last train home.

The same psychic (Maelgwn/David) who had guided me to the spot where I awoke the sleepers at Beltaine soon came through with a message for me. If Derfel wished to find Tegfedd in this life, I should do certain things. I was told that Derfel and Tegfedd had been lovers (and cousins). Tegfedd had escaped indoctrination by Illtyd and had the reputation of being a witch, following the Celtic and druidical spiritual path rather than the dogma of the Roman church and its patriarchal priests. Tegfedd had not wanted the battle of Camlan to take place. She was torn between loyalty to her lover Derfel and her Uncle Arthur. Illtyd's Roman party included her elder brother Samson (Old Dry Lip), although she barely knew him. Tegfedd had

26

attended to the wounded on the hillside of Bryn Cleifion and to the dying King Arthur when he was brought to the chapel at Mallwyd. She had followed Arthur's body to Ynys Enlli (Bardsey Island), then Ynys Byr

(Caldey Island) and, finally, to a woodland cave (near the River Wye?). Back in her mother's homeland of Gwent she made her hermit's cell at the place now bearing her name. Her neighbours were suspicious of her, calling her a witch, especially when it became obvious she was pregnant. Derfel had eventually found out where Tegfedd was and had joined her, building his chapel a few miles to the west in what to him was a strange and hostile land. He had no other reason to be there. Maelgwn Gwynedd, the new pendragon, even paid a secret visit.

The oak and the wren
Now the spirit of Maelgwn Gwynedd was telling me through David Evans that Derfel would soon see a sign marking the start of his Quest. This would be in the form of a brown-grey speckled bird. Within one month after that, he would meet Tegfedd, who was both near him at times and away in the borderlands. Her physical description was given, as was the fact that she was very Celtic. I was to take her to Aberdyfi beach as soon as possible. I would know her by 'the oak and the wren'. I was to summon her by collecting a 'male' stone and a 'female' stone from Bryn Cleifion, where Tegfedd had nursed the wounded and observed the battle. I was to take the 'male' stone to Tegfedd's church, the 'female' stone to the ruins of Derfel's chapel, to leave bread as an offering to the birds at both places and to pray at both spots that Derfel and Tegfedd would be re-united in this world in the present. The modern Tegfedd would help me write the true story of Camlan.

The sacred cuckoo
I hesitated, not knowing if I wanted to get involved. I also didn't have the money to take another trip to Cwmbrân. I went to Carn Ingli to tape-record the dreams of Sir Bedwyr and his wife Rhonwen and they were with me as

27

I took down the tent on Saturday morning, 25th May, 1996. As I was dealing with the tent on the mountain I know to be sacred to Rhiannon, a cuckoo circled around and around my head, swooping low. The dreamers with me pointed out that it was obviously trying to make itself known to me. They did not know

of my Quest. I have never seen a cuckoo at the summit of Carn Ingli before or since (I have spent over one thousand nights there) and did not know this bird possessed the grey-brown speckled belly that would be a sign to me. The way it drew my attention was so strange and obvious that when I had time in Aberystwyth between buses on the way home that afternoon I browsed in Siop y Pethe bookshop. I had long fancied a book on Celtic animal totems by Miranda Green at a price I could not afford. I meant to look up cuckoo in it. When I reached out to the shelf I found my hand picking up another book next to it instead. This was a book on Welsh folklore which seemed to leap at me. It fell open at a page which was all about .... cuckoos! I read that the cuckoo was a bird sacred to Rhiannon and that seeing it marked the start of a spiritual quest. When I did turn to Miranda Green's book, it had nothing in it about cuckoos.

Later that same day, as I walked between home and office, I went up Bryn Cleifion and immediately found a 'male' stone and a 'female' stone. Now I had to go back to Cwmbrân. As it happened, George was driving me to Carn Ingli on Monday, 3rd June, then onto Ilfracombe the next day *(Tuesday 4th June),* where we had arranged to take the ferry to Lundy. There are many strands to the story woven by the dreams on Carn Ingli. (An earlier dream told me I must go to Lundy and when I returned home there was an offer of a free press trip to Lundy for myself and a partner). I didn't tell George what my purpose was, but I asked him to divert off the motorway for an hour that Tuesday so that I could visit Capel Derfel and Llantegfedd.

The holy grail comes to Wales
We didn't have much time and I couldn't find Capel Derfel because new roads and houses had put my map out of date. Knocking on a door, the first person I asked was the retired farmer who used to own the land on which the ruins stand. We quickly found Capel Derfel and summoned Tegfedd. Reaching Llantegfedd, we gained the key this time and opened

28

the door to see an exhibition of Sunday School paintings about the holy grail. Later I learnt how Derfel had carried the holy grail, the chalice used by Jesus at the Last Supper, from Glastonbury to the Strata Florida area of Ceredigion. He had not known what it was. He merely carried it on behalf of the nine maidens who guard it, from the Chalice Well, Glastonbury, west and away from the Saxons. It is now known as the Nanteos Cup. He also escorted a pregnant lady (Tegfedd?) on the Gwent section of this trip. The holy grail could also refer to the pregnant womb, especially the bloodline of Jesus, as Laurence Gardner writes about in *'Bloodline of the Holy Grail'* (pub. Element, 1996) – a book that wasn't published until five months later in November, 1996.

Whilst Derfel was away on this task in Ceredigion, Tegfedd was killed. I discovered two versions of her death. One blamed a band of marauding Saxons, with the reverent locals erecting a chapel in Tegfedd's memory at the spot she died. That was the official version for the returning and soon to be grieving Derfel. The other story was that the locals couldn't understand why Tegfedd was so generous to the poor, so they stoned her to death for being a witch (and a pregnant one at that). Years later dreams revealed the truth contained in my *'Dream of Derfel'* (see later). Having summoned Tegfedd here, too, George and I continued to Lundy.

Postcard from the past
After Lundy, I fasted for one week at the summit of Cadair Idris and went to Carn Ingli for the summer solstice, where I was told the holy grail descended upon me while I slept (Maelgwn/David's explanation of a light witnessed over me by a lady from Glastonbury on the night of Wednesday, 19th June). I returned to my office on Friday, 21st June and received a postcard on the 22nd June, from a lady called Lisa who had my book *'In the Footsteps of King Arthur'* and wanted to discuss it with me. Her postcard was a picture of horses and she had written that hers was the silver one – what colour was mine? I took this to be a sign from the goddess Rhiannon. Telephoning her, she arrived promptly after a long car journey the next morning at 9 am, Sunday, 23rd June, 1996 (I didn't know then this was the anniversary of Camlan).

The oak and the wren revealed
Lisa's first words to me were, 'I have come to help you write'. She then said, 'Please can we go to Aberdyfi beach?' She looked like the person I was expecting. She then gave me a booklet of her poems and I noticed that her pen-name was Elisabeth Oakland. I would know Tegfedd by 'the oak'! I then came to a strange drawing facing the poem to the 'spent

warrior' (which mentions a she-wolf prowling at my door on 26th March, when I did have a she-wolf in my tent on Carn Ingli). I asked Lisa what the picture was and she rotated the page to reveal a wren! I had the oak, the wren, Aberdyfi beach, the person who would help me write and she looked the part. Lisa came from the border area, Gloucestershire, where she is known as being very Celtic (teaching herself Welsh). Owning a caravan in Ceredigion, Lisa was actually shopping in Cardigan when George and I were doing the same on our way to Carn Ingli on Monday, 3rd June, so we had been close to each other without realising – probably on many occasions.

Only later did I tell her about Tegfedd. She had come because she wanted to write a book about King Arthur. Her mother had given her a copy of my book *'In the Footsteps of King Arthur'* for her birthday, on *Tuesday, 4th June*, the very day I summoned Tegfedd with my prayers and offerings at Capel Derfel and Llantegfedd. As if all this wasn't conclusive evidence, Lisa also gave me a poem which she said she felt was especially relevant. It follows and its title incorporates the druidic chant *I A A I E O*, which Arthur first taught me when he knighted me on Carn Ingli. She wrote it early in the morning of Monday, 27th May, 1996, after a sleepless night. This was shortly after the start of my spiritual quest on Saturday, 25th May, 1996, the day when I also collected the 'male' and 'female' stones from Bryn Cleifion and determined to summon Tegfedd.

30

I A J A I E O

I remembered you as soon as I heard your voice
I recognised you as soon as I saw your face
I knew who you were before I even knocked on your door
But only dimly.
You awoke the stirring psyche I carried inside me
Your voice more powerful than I expected it to be
Your thoughts of me sweeter than ever before
Disguised thinly.
At once I knew you as a long lost one
Slowly I saw you were a mighty son
In a revelation I saw the task that had begun
And took it gratefully.
No burden is too heavy when you know your mind
No weight of past times cannot be gladly left behind
No failure is a failure when all is said and done
If accepted gracefully.
A past failure accepted is a learning tool
A past success is a temptation to be a fool
A past past is by far the happiest state
Accepted knowingly.
We all have maps of where we have been in our heads
We all have blueprints in our minds of where we shall tread
We all think we would like to know our own Fate
And would accept it willingly.
Do not go to fortune tellers, do not cross their palms with silver
Do not pay the gypsy, tell her you are like her,
Do not heed the careless words of others;
Know only your own mind.
Instead take the silver of your hands, heart and tongue
Instead search for your own task; it is already begun
Instead find your own way in life, and search for brothers;
They are there to find.
I remembered you dimly but now the memory shines
You may remember me, but it must be in your own time
What you are to me I do not ask you to see;
Let us both just Be.

Elisabeth Oakland 27.5.1996
IAAIEO, 5 and 8

31

From Elisabeth Oakland *(Lisa/Tegfedd)*   July, 1997

I contacted Laurence Main because my mother gave me *'In the Footsteps of King Arthur'* for my birthday; she was aware of my longstanding interest in the subject and that I was in the process of producing a leaflet about the local King Arthur connection in Gloucestershire.

I had recently read several life-changing books, notably Robert Bly's *'Iron John'*, Robert Graves' *'The White Goddess'* and Mary Caine's *'The Glastonbury Zodiac – Key to the Mysteries of Britain'*. These all combined to present a coherent initiation into the language of myth and symbolism, and enhanced, reinforced and helped me interpret my simultaneous spiritual awakening. If given the chance, psychologists might explain it all away as an adjustment episode, but my own explanation works much better for me, because I *know* it is true; after reading Robert Bly's book, I dedicated myself to the moon, as a symbol of womanhood, thus instinctively and unwittingly linking in with a huge, powerful source of knowledge, the Jungian 'collective unconscious', but that is another story........

So it was that, by this time a master of 'constructive foot-following', I went with my strong intuition that Laurence was someone I should meet; the outcome, as already described by Laurence, bears out how right I was to trust that instinct. The modern day events Laurence describes in this book really happened. Whether they prove the reality of reincarnation, psychic phenomena, genetic memory, the goddess or a combination of all these factors is a question of interpretation and, above all, faith: belief is a choice, faith is a deep inner conviction: believe what you must, but open your mind and, if you do not already, you can *know* faith.

The Nanteos Cup

After the publication of *'Camlan – The True Story?'* in 1997, I gave talks and sold booklets. I was soon contacted by a lady concerned with the safekeeping of the Nanteos Cup, the holy grail carried by Derfel. Dreams had alerted her to my coming, then a friend had heard my talk and bought the booklet. Early in 1998 I was taken in a series of cars, switching at remote locations to avoid detection, to see the Nanteos Cup. Lisa/Tegfedd was allowed to join me. In October, 1999, whilst walking near Strata Florida I felt sure the holy well Derfel took the holy grail to was nearby. I write about its discovery in my book *'The Spirit Paths of Wales'* (Cicerone Press). I visited it in 2000 with M. (Eurgain/Spirit of Deganwy), finding it by dowsing. Pat/Enddwyn visited it with me in 2001. I believe both were in the reception party in late 537.

Good saints, bad saints and a virtuous woman

Rosetta, an American lady, contacted me in 1998, as I have expanded on in *'The Spirit Paths of Wales'*. Led by her own vivid dreams, she knew herself to be the reincarnation of St Gwladus, wife of Gwynlliw (Sir Lancelot) and mother of St Catwg (Cadoc/Sir Galahad). Selling her bookshop in the USA to fund regular research trips to Wales, our paths soon crossed and we were companions on our Quests. In November, 1999, Rosetta surprised me by sending a copy of *'Saints, Knights and Llannau'*, an obscure Arthurian book by T. Thornley Jones, published by Gomer Press in 1975. I was completely unaware of this book until then. On page 62 in it was the statement that Tegfedd (sister of Tydecho) *'seems to have found a champion in Derfel, son of Hywel Mawr the grandson of Emyr Llydaw'*. I have no idea why this author made this statement. I contacted Gomer Press, but they had no contact address for T.Thornley Jones now.

In late 2000 coincidence brought me into contact with Gaenor, whose dreams and experiences suggest she is the reincarnation of Trynihid, according to Sabine Baring-Gould and J. Fisher 'a virtuous woman' who suffered from being Illtyd's wife. In their entry on 'St' Illtyd they record how the misogynist treated her cruelly, then abandoned her. Trynihid might have served as a matron for the boys (including Derfel) at Illtyd's college in Llantwit Major.

Expecting 'angel-face'

Gradually the story that follows in *'The Dream Of Derfel'* emerged. My own recollections of Camlan grew, while Maelgwn/David's dreams contributed. One morning he telephoned to warn me to expect Sandde Angel-face. I

happened to be leading an advertised walk that day around Camlan. The previous year (it was part of Machynlleth's annual festival) a whole bus-load had turned up. This year there was only one person, a man with an angelic face. A healer, he took my dowsing rods when at Arthur's memorial stone and traced the ley all the way to the altar at St Tydecho's Church, Mallwyd. The walk was abandoned whilst he soaked up the atmosphere of a place he'd never been to before in this life but had suddenly felt drawn to. I didn't spoil things by telling him what I knew and certainly didn't mention Sandde. He was most grateful for having being brought back to a place he now felt had great significance to him, however. I gave him a copy of *'Camlan – the True Story?'* to read on the bus back to Machynlleth.

Whilst fasting at the summit of Carn Ingli in late May, 2002, two horses made their way to my tent. Rocks made this extremely difficult to do and in over one thousand nights there I've never witnessed this except that 26th May. The date was Maelgwn/David's birthday in this life. The horses grazed gently around my tent. One was black (Maelgwn's) and the other was grey (Derfel's).

Poisoned by a scheming snake charmer
Maelgwn/David's dreams were clear that Illtyd caused Camlan by convincing Arthur to invade Gwynedd. It was a civil war involving reluctant participants. Only Illtyd's scheming, poisoned words and the use of an adder at the crucial moment made it happen. There is a clear figure of forty thousand involved. Camlan was a massive battle involving men from far and near. The Saxon mercenaries were Arthur's. If you think the average warband numbered only three hundred, consider that *'The Welsh Triads'* numbers 29 and 30 refer to Gabran (of Dal Riada) and Alan Fyrgan each having warbands of *'twenty-one hundred men'*. Most of the fighting took

34

place at Maes y Camlan and as Derfel taunted Arthur to extend his army by chasing him up Cwm Cerist. The tide of battle turned at the Camlan near Bwlch Oerddrws (*SH 821 169*), as Arthur's extended army was ambushed, then fled back to Maes y Camlan. Arthur received his mortal wound near the head of Cwm Cerist but expired in his nephew's church at Mallwyd in the arms of his niece, Tegfedd. Derfel and Bedwyr were there too.

Mystical tool

Whilst Derfel dealt with the bulk of the fighting in Mawddwy, Illtyd was craftily outflanking the main battle by landing with a small force in the Mawddach estuary (at Llanelltyd). Fog had enabled his boats to elude Gabran's Dal Riadan fleet. Illtyd had already established himself at Llanelltyd because he knew it to be the Pole Star, the pointed end of Ursa Minor (cf Mike Harris' Cadair Idris star map in '*The Cauldron*' no 118). This was the end of a mystic tool controlling the land. Illtyd (and Rome) always sought control through fear. Maelgwn (the hound prince) knew to concentrate on foiling Illtyd's plan and defeated Illtyd's men in the Ganllwyd Cwm Camlan (*SH 715 246*), thus preventing Illtyd 'grasping the handle' to make effective use of this mystical tool in the landscape. Seemingly a minor skirmish in a long day, whilst Arthur was engaged in Mawddwy, the Ganllwyd episode was of immense mystical significance.

Tomb, womb and vengeance

Similarly, the body of Arthur had to rest at Arthog (*SH 643 145*) in the Corona Borealis, the bear's cave (womb/tomb) before going to Ynys Enlli / Bardsey / Isle of Apples. Bardsey is still famous for its ancient strain of apple. Illtyd later claimed the body and it ended up in a secret woodland cave (Lisa/Tegfedd's dream showed such a scene without any clue to its

35

maintain his power) and had Tegfedd killed. Derfel then killed Illtyd in revenge. Visiting the scene of Illtyd's death at Bedd Gwyl Illtyd (*SN 977 264* on OS Explorer OL 12) in February, 2001, with Rosetta (on a trip from the USA) we defied the Old Ill-tide to do his worst. A mighty wind almost (but not quite) blew out our candle, the sky darkened and the Foot and Mouth Disease was first reported that evening. Its centre in Wales (until that December) was a nearby farm at Libanus. As a guidebook writer, I was very nearly ruined by the restrictions imposed on walkers (and, unlike farmers, was not compensated).

Maelgwn's last words
Maelgwn/David asked me to perform a ritual for him at the summit of Cadair Idris in May, 2003. That night I dreamt of slipping on orange peel and eating red kidney beans. I then descended to the Moot of the 'Society of Leyhunters' in Corris Youth Hostel. The last telephone call from Maelgwn/David was brief (I was busy entertaining ley hunters). Maelgwn/David said the Moot would go well (it did), Derfel's Rhiannon would attend it (she did) and eventually after a great test of patience, Rhiannon would return to Derfel. I would know this by 'the two red kites'. Rhiannon did send me a postcard thanking me for the Moot. Its picture was of two red kites.........

Early on Monday morning after that Moot, on 12th May, my daughter's cat acted in a uniquely strange way. It woke me up by kissing and licking me. I glanced at the clock. It was 4.53 am. About 9 am I received a telephone call from Maelgwn/David's brother. David had died at 4.53 am.

Phone call from the dead
This incident reminded me of December, 1983, when I received a telephone call from Jack Sanderson, President of the Vegan Society and Chairman of the Society for Psychical Research. I was then working as Assistant Secretary of the Vegan Society. Jack made a strange, jocular telephone call at 7.30 am. Not long afterwards, by 8 am, Kathleen Jannaway, Hon. Secretary of the Vegan Society, telephoned to tell me Jack Sanderson had died during the night. As proof of survival of the soul, this was not needed by me. All my life I have *known* the truth of reincarnation.

'Spirit of Deganwy' answers
In 1999, Maelgwn/David urged me when in great distress to call upon the 'Spirit of Deganwy'. This I did that December. The next day a woman telephoned me from a local nature reserve inviting me to lead walks on the theme of local history alongside the Dyfi Estuary. I referred to Traeth

36

Maelgwn as we discussed local places of interest. The woman (M.) said that Maelgwn was her hero. 'Why?' I asked. 'I'm from Deganwy', M. said. She also drew a picture whilst at school of a king, inspired by her interest in historical characters from ages past from the surrounding area of Deganwy, her home. The picture appears on page 37. Every day whilst at school in Conwy, she would gaze across the river to the enigmatic hill known locally as *'The Vardre'* (where Maelgwn held his court) and day-dream about knights, princesses, princes and folk from other times who would have lived there. She grew up less than a mile from the site of his court.

Proof of goddess worship

Dreams soon revealed M. was my *'Spirit of Deganwy'* and the reincarnation of Eurgain, the daughter of Maelgwn and his chosen heiress. M. and I dreamt on the crown of the profile of a landscape goddess, part of the 'Vardre' at Deganwy, in early March, 2000. M. dreamt of a word – 'Elevis'. We returned to my house, to the postman bringing me a review copy of a book by Paul Devereux, *'The Illustrated Encyclopedia of Ancient Earth Mysteries'.* It literally fell open on the page containing the account of Eleusis, the place in Greece where ancient rituals, pilgrimage and ceremonies were carried out in the name of the goddess Demeter. Then M.'s mother sent a cutting from her local *'Weekly News'*, dated 30th March, 2000. It revealed archaeological findings that Caer Seion on Conwy Mountain (across the estuary from Deganwy) was a temple to the goddess.

Her priestesses correspond to the Greek Furies and were linked to Maelgwn Gwynedd's castle at Deganwy. Was this the link with Eleusis? King Maelgwn's princess would have been a high priestess. Dreams and events leave me in no doubt that M., Spirit of Deganwy, was Maelgwn's eldest daughter, Princess Eurgain.

'Eurgain, daughter of Maelgwn Gwynedd, who set the candle to the wild birds, in order to show the way to her lover'.

38

CAMLAN

At Camlan many gathered,
Many strong in arm and heart;
Strong in body, weak in spirit.
Camlan saw many great men,
Great was the host, long was the strife.
Maelgwn and Arthur, great kings;
Long their shadows on the land:
The grey king, dragon-hearted.
The dragon banner raised thrice,
The head dragon disputed twice,
The great Bear a raven's wing.
Long wives weep, long the memory;
Internecine strife: the fool's war.
At Camlan, who gathered ?
In the field, the horde of Sais,
On the mount, the poet band,
By the ford, Maelgwn's men arrayed.
Great the fear of those who knew
To die today was to be reborn:
A midwife of futility: Camlan.
Strong men rose up as milkmaids;
Great kings, heads not high,
As many years as those who died
Sleep not well in their halls
Beneath the hills, but fitfully.
Wrongful war: the conscience of ages:
Camlan.

Elisabeth Oakland, 1997

39

The Dream of Derfel

David Darvel Gatheren,
As sayeth the Welshman,
Fetched outlaws out of Hell;
Now is he come with spear and shield,
In harness to burne in Smithfeld,
For in Wales he may not dwel.

And Forest the Freer,
That obstinate lyer,
That wilfully shal be dead,
In his contumacye
The Gospel doeth deny,
The Kyng to be supreme heade.

(Hall's Chronicles, 22nd May, 1538)

And I, Derfel, dreamt as I lay,
Knowing I have not long to stay,
In this breeze and under these stars,
At the top of Mynydd Enlli,
Seeing my statue's destiny,
Adding timber to holy fires.
A scene from a distant future,
When the king would be a Tudor,
Seemed so strange yet well meant for me.

My gaze is to the south at dawn,
Along a coast where mountains form,
To where I perceive Carn Ingli.
On my left the land of Maelgwn,
Where there was fighting at Camlan,
When Gwent's Arthur rode against we.
Reflecting on such stirring times,
Spirit calls me to write these lines,
For I must record
my story........

Born far across the sea by fate,
In four hundred and ninety-eight
Of Our lord the prophet Jesse,
In the sun-kissed land of Llydaw,
Where grandad Budic was Emyr
And young Guyar was my granny.
Pity about that brat Medrawt,
Whose father was Guyar's brother,
That is young King Arthur, you see.
The arrangement pleased old Budic,
To have a new, young, buxom wife,
He soon fell dead most happily.
His son Hywel was my father
And Pompeia was my mother,
Being Hywel's noble good wife.
Guyar then went north to her Lot,
Gawain, or Gwalchmai, she begot,
Dragging Medrawt out of my life.
And so I next remember school,
Under old Ill-tide's harshest rule,
On the Silures' southern shore.
Illtyd, holy servant of Rome,
Having taken me far from home,
Did his utmost a boy to bore.
The Jesus he beat into us
Was not the one my mother's trust
Had taught me, when young, to adore.
When I protested, as I can,
But she is only a woman!
Cried the 'saint' that I did abhore.

42

But even worse, ought you to know,
Than when old Ill-tide's stick did throw,
Were his hands upon our young knees.
I did resist ev'ry advance
And only offered a stern glance,
But Taliesin did him please.
One night I found Maelgwn in fear
As Illtyd aimed hard at his rear
And the 'saint' fled, no doubt to pray.
I packed our things and fetched my horse
To rescue my school friend, of course,
And we fled from Illtyd that day.
With Maelgwn clinging to my back,
Under the moon, along the track
White snow lay as we rode my Grey.

The Via Julia went west
Towards my father's new estate,
Then for Gwynedd we made our way.
I left Maelgwn with Cadwallon
And returned to Hywel's new home
In the land of the Demetii.
Hywel spoke of war in Llydaw
Thus causing him here to withdraw,
So protecting our family.
'Twas the year five hundred and twelve
I learnt with lance and sword to delve
As a warrior called to fight.
You can ride so far and so fast,
Surely as a knight you are cast,
Said Arthur by the fire at night.
In Llydaw we carous'd with mirth
To defend the land of my birth
Against hostile Andecavi.
So I rode in Hywel's warband
To teach invaders of our land
That British it would always be.
The start of my story of woe
Came one dawn, surprising our foe,
When I bravely saved Sadurn's life.
Sadurn pushed a girl towards me,
Saying my reward she would be,
Though I need not make her my wife.
Into a dark hut we were shut,
Two virgins so together put,
Whilst grown men laughed loudly outside.

I tried to put my arms around
The girl who sobbed without a sound,
For she was plainly terrified.
War makes men cruel and obscene
But in the darkness we stayed clean.
In the morning she was taken
To an unknown fate by others
Who treated her less like brothers
And so innocence was broken.
This I still feel deeply inside
That a girl is not merchandise;
I should have done more for her sake.
A warrior enough to kill,
Yet bound to do my elders' will,
Next time my protests I would make.
Ordered by Hywel and Arthur
Back to Britain's shore for more war,
To me these were exciting times.
The Saxons of Osla Big Knife
Had come with Cerdic to cause strife,
Advancing on our British lines.
Life was simple, with a purpose,
Defeat them or they would kill us.
Along Ermine Street to Lindum
For some fighting not far from there,
Back south and west to the fort where
Flowed the Bassas, Letocetum.
To Minerva's shrine I was brought,
Where blessings from Brigit were sought.
The goddess helped me in that fight,

We won, a truce was realised
And to Hywel's and my surprise
Arthur raised me up as a knight.
A boundary had been agreed,
So now our king had greatest need
For rangers to patrol its line.
To face the Saxons, most rode east
On black horses, a section each.
Further south, near Cerdic was mine.
Before going where I would roam
I was allowed to return home
With Hywel to the Demetii.
At last I would my sisters see,
Enddwyn and Helen (called Lene),
Oh, what peace and joy this would be.

Riding my grey horse to the sea,
One morning I had company.
Out of the waves stepped a maiden,
Naked and slim with long, dark hair,
She proudly walked with her chest bare,
A girl of my age, how brazen.
She walked boldly up to my side,
Stroked my horse and asked for a ride.
This goddess was called Rhiannon.

She was one of the Demetii
Who lived not far away from me
And a spirited young woman.
Daily we swam, we rode, we walked,
We embraced, we kissed and we talked,
Rhiannon, will you marry me?
Yes, Derfel, when it's time I will,
Words spoken on our holy hill........
I pause to look at Carn Ingli.

For warriors, duty soon calls
To take us away from our halls.
With Hywel I had to ride north,
At Deva's fortress to muster
In the service of King Arthur.
We would show what Britons are worth.

47

Maelgwn, I was most glad to see,
Had come to ride along side me
At the head of men from Gwynedd.
Telling Maelgwn of Rhiannon,
My friend thought she was a good one.
How different from old Illtyd.
Tempting maidens at our feet fell,
Maelgwn was too shy I could tell,
Whilst my heart had now been taken.

Sawyl Penuchel joined us then
With warriors from Elmet when
We stopped at Bremetenacum.
His family had come with him,
For Saxons were at Elmet's rim
And Maelgwn's eyes on Nesta fell.
He spent his time under the trees
With Sawyl's daughter on his knees,
My friend had found love, I could tell.

For Caledonia we rose
Where painted Picts suffered our blows
Although we were not yet fifteen.
With Mary painted on his shield
(some say a goddess he did wield)
Arthur's mighty strength we had seen.
With Saxons and Picts in dismay,
Forest and old castle made way
To the road for Eboracum.
South our triumphal progress went,
We sang of riding down to Kent,
I guarding our rear with Maelgwn.
Sawyl Penuchel was well met
As he approached his land, Elmet,
Where 'Reet champion' was the cry.
We approached Legiolium,
With thoughts of relaxation,
When behind us I did espy
The Saxons – the Saxons – are here,
I warned Arthur – towards our rear!
Despite combat, I did not die.
A victory, but it was clear
Arthur's army could not leave here,
At Bremetenacum we'd lie.
Flushing Saxons from the woodlands
Onto the estuary sands,
The Ribble soon with blood did flow.
Once again we came to Deva,
Where Maelgwn left Princess Nesta,
And I went south with Hywel now,

To Cerdic's border we did ride
Alongside Arthur with great pride
South to our pendragon's homeland,
Where we at Bregion surprised
Traitor Cerdic and his allies
Daring on Arthur's ground to stand,
They thought up north we would have lost
But they soon found out to their cost
That we were seasoned warriors.
The border was again agreed,
To patrol it was now my need,
As ordered by superiors.
To Aquae Sulis I first went,
Where into great baths I was sent,
And I met a girl named Helen.
She took me to the sacred spring
Where goddess Sulis called me in
And I remembered Rhiannon.
I too have loved, oh Derfel dear,
But death took my hero from here,
Said Helen, servant of Sulis.
When you ride south to the border,
May I come as your visitor?
And so we rode at June's solstice
To where a river eastward flowed
From green upland, windswept and wild
And a temple stood on a hill.
A man we met grew watercress
And with battle tales was impressed,
He pronounced my name Deveril.

With Helen gone, I pitched my tent
For now my time here would be spent,
Cerdic's frontier to ride along.
'Til I was surprised one fine day
By Helen riding down my way
With none other than Rhiannon.
My love did stay inside my tent,
Together with Hywel's consent,
We explored under a blue sky
To the belly of goddess Sul
And rings of stone below her hill,
Before my love bade me goodbye.

A poem from Rhiannon to Derfel, autumn, 513:

I love you for yourself,
just as you are —
for your simpleness
and humility
and your faith in God.
And as I love you
'Tis not just my love
that I give to you,
but love that
comes from the Source
and flows through me to you,
And in our loving each other,
To the Source may it return.

Time came when I was seventeen,
Allowed back home and oh so keen
For my wedding to Rhiannon.
Old Dyfrig came to be the priest
At the sunny summer solstice,
The year five hundred and fifteen.
Wearing white flowers on her head,
In the sacred circle of trees
Later to be called Llanrhian.

Maelgwn came and gave me a sword,
Goblet embossed, engraved in gold
As a present for Rhiannon.

Bliss takes no account of time,
Even the rain seems soft and fine,
Every tree is in its place
And bees go buzzing happily.
Dolphins take leaps out of the sea,
Whilst rabbits in the fields do race.
Your love is there, simply is there,
Ev'ry wonderful thing to share
Contentedly around evening fires.
Then, wondrous joy, the news is told
That we will soon a baby hold,
Before next Saint John's Eve bonfires.

As time sped forth to our great day
Fate cruelly took me away
To defend our British Kingdom
Against Saxon Osla Big Knife
And traitor Cerdic in the south –
I had to leave my Rhiannon.
My wife gave me a warm embrace
But distant eyes glowed in her face
As I rode with Hywel's warband.
I had not ridden very far
When came from Cadwallon Lawhir
A messenger from Gwynedd's land.

Maelgwn was keen with us to ride
But first came his family pride
Of his handfasting to Nesta.
The parties were in residence
And to postpone would cause offence,
So to Deganwy would I go?
Hywel pondered for a moment,
Realised that reinforcements
Would return with me from the north.
Men from both Gwynedd and Elmet,
Even Powys, if we well met
When by Sarn Helen I rode forth.
With best shield and finest linen
Bought by me from Moridunum
And water fresh from Mabon's cave,
The handfasting I reached in time;
Next day Maelgwn's men rode with mine
And Maelgwn his honeymoon gave
To perform his royal duty
For his honour, not for booty,
Far from home to serve his country.
So we rode, old friends together,
To ask Owain Ddantgwyn whether
Powys would to Arthur rally.
Maelgwn's uncle quickly agreed
To his nephew's most urgent need,
But declined to join in person.
With swollen ranks I met Hywel
That hot June in the town of Sul,
Young men keen to face the Saxon.

Maelgwn came with me on patrol,
Over looking the White Horse Vale,
Expecting Osla from the east.
I felt sure that an invader
Would take the road from Calleva
Up the valley of the Cunnit
So I King Arthur had prepared
When Osla's Saxon Army stared
At us from the hill of Badon.
Maelgwn held Arthur's red dragon
While I hoisted Gwynedd's gold one
And Arthur cut down the Saxon.
Cerdic came late, soon turned and fled,
Along Ridgeway were strewn the dead
And Aquae Sulis, it was saved.
On Saint John's long day this was seen
In year five hundred and sixteen.
Then soon my presence it was waived,
Home to Rhiannon I was sent,
To Nesta, Maelgwn Gwynedd went,
I rode west with all my young life,
With hopeful thoughts that our baby
Would now be there for me to see,
Beside Rhiannon, my dear wife.

Dark and gloomy the western sky
As homeward rode my Grey and I
Into thunder and bright lightning.
Riding on with the greatest care
To reach our hut, where to my stare
A strange woman was breastfeeding.
My mother and sisters appeared,
Weeping tears and me gently steered
To the fresh grave of Rhiannon.
My wife died after giving birth
To our son, whose name we chose Nerth,
Now suckling from a strange woman.
In our sacred grove I lay down
Beside white flowers on her mound
And remembered last year's wedding.
Rhiannon's face and sparkling eyes,
Her free spirit, so young yet wise,
And the warmth of our lovemaking.
My love died on the very day
Hundreds were cut down by the way
At the battle of Mount Badon.
I wish that death had sought me then
So that I had joined my love when
Struggle of birth killed Rhiannon.
I did not want to leave her grave,
Would not be a warrior brave,
For what was now left to live for?
When Nerth cried, I could not him feed
And thus provide his greatest need,
My heart was stricken to the core.

I took to roaming far from home,
Feeding birds as if they had come
From my darling departed one,
To the summit of Carn Ingli,
Where my true love's spirit would be,
While a strange woman fed our son.
Through autumn, winter, even spring,
A new year relief could not bring,
So I chose to await my death
Without food on our holy hill,
Rhiannon's face my dreams did fill,
As I prayed hard for my last breath.
One day I awoke from a dream
Where I crossed a lake, it did seem,
To meet friends on a mountain path.
Witnessing a golden sunrise,
Two red kites flew above my eyes
And I rose, leaning on my staff.

Arising from my weakened state,
As if drawn by the hand of fate,
My eyes were most surprised to see
Maelgwn Gwynedd on his black horse
With my Grey following their course
Stepping o'er the rocks to reach me.
Oh Derfel, Derfel, will you live?
Your armed assistance to me give?
Uncle Owain Odantgwyn must die.
Cadwallon my father is dead,
Killed by his brother in his bed,
Who dares to blame me with a lie.
With you at my side, we will win
And purge Powys of Owain's sin
To confound his conspiracy.
Elmet, under Nesta's father
And fiery Oechtir, her mother,
Challenge Owain's supremacy.
Domangort of Dal Riada
With young Gabran will come after
To help the son of their ally.
We both fought against the Irish
Who tried to take Mona's Ynys –
Cadwallon helped them loyally.
Maelgwn, I lay down here to die
But death can be postponed till I
Have helped you to gain your kingdom.
With luck I might even be slain
Upon a mountain, moor or plain,
Freeing me to join Rhiannon.

And so north to Gwynedd we rode
As in those schoolboy days of old
To fight for truth and what is right.

Who can strew whiteness in summer while
rivers run red ?
Can Gwyn ap Nudd counting his fishes and
furling his sails ?
No! They're for Derfel, for Derfel,
these dainty dead;
Stripped of their armour, like mackerel
Stripped of their scales!

John Cowper Powys (in his 'Owen Glendower')

When Owain fell, Powys took fright,
They had no stomach for a fight,
Cuneglasus lay down his arms.
I will atone for treachery
And be your ally most gladly
Swore Owain's son, Maelgwn's cousin.

59

With Gwynedd and Powys at peace
Came a Christian wedding feast,
Coronation for king and queen
In splendour at Deganwy seen,
Maelgwn in purple, Nesta green,
Year five hundred and seventeen.

So in Gwynedd I found myself,
To serve my friend, not seeking wealth,
The kingdom would need defending.
With death so near, saints soon appear,
Led by my cousins without fear,
Holy rights and land demanding.
Maelgwn said, Remember Ill-tide,
All saints do not by God abide,
Let us test their undertaking.
Derfel, your cousin Tydecho
On our border has settled, so
A visit there let's be paying.
We ride south to Mawddwy's valley,
Shaped like a womb in a belly,
Land most sacred to the goddess,
Mawdd or Ceridwen her name be,
Tydecho's nature we must see,
He will have to prove his goodness.

We had been to school together
And Tydecho's elder brother
Was one of Ill-tide's boys, Samson.
But he came here with young Tegfedd,
A pagan unloved by Illtyd,
Now becoming a fair maiden.
If a false Roman Maelgwn found,
Tydecho would flee from our hounds,
If the goddess he knew to serve,
White horses would on mountains feed
And wild beasts would help meet his needs.
Wild stags and wolf we did observe
Plough Dol y Ceirw as livestock,
Maelgwn stuck fast upon a rock,
Until the saint released our king
For privilege of sanct'ary
And maids enjoying liberty
In church where they God's praises sing,
To be for one hundred ages,
As recorded upon pages.
My memory was of the maid,
Pretty Tegfedd, niece of Arthur,
Daughter of Ammun and Anna,
For whom a dowry would be paid.

In year five hundred and nineteen
Double celebration was seen
At Maelgwn's court in Deganwy.
Baby Princess Eurgain was born
To Queen Nesta and King Maelgwn
Before my twenty-first birthday.
Still alone, I shared my friend's joy,
We both minded not for a boy,
The feast was held in a great hall.
Wine from far Constantinople
Had come, to please other people
Since such drink was not for my call,
Then came a sight to mark my age,
An exotic dancer took stage
Who had come all the way from Thrace.
Her name was Anna, a princess
Captured and sold, to her distress,
When I saw her my heart did race.
Her hair was long, curly and dark,
Skin tanned, waist slim, her dancing art,
Could I enjoy life once again?
Then Maelgwn stood to tell his court
That as a surprise he had bought
For my birthday a concubine.
Anna joined me in my round hut
Forbidden to marry me but
I treated her as my good wife.
We lived above the crashing sea
On Ynys Mon, near Caergybi,
Where wild Irish raiders were rife.

Gwynedd's border was mine to guard,
In time I knew every yard –
Maelgwn trusted defence to me.
A baby ev'ry other year,
Bringing Anna and I great cheer,
Glad our sixth child we would soon see.
Sometimes I was called far away
By Dal Riada, our ally,
And thus fate had in store for me
That sailing home, I found my wife
And five children deprived of life,
Killed by men from across the sea.

In Maelgwn's service I remained,
Cwm Bowydd my own court retained,
'Tho I found it an empty hall.

Neither did I often visit
Deganwy and the court in it
Where politics' intrigue did call.
Orc's Mynach sang Maelgwn's praises,
For Picts he fathered princesses,
As part of his royal duty.
Maelgwn, my friend, I knew to be
A servant of his people's needs,
Which to him were counted holy.
Thus testing saints gave him ill-fame
When they took revenge on his name
Despite his generosity.
My choice was to guard the border
And keep old Cedig in order
Where Sarn Helen crossed the Dyfi.
He soon left me a young widow,
Tegfedd, sister of Tydecho,
Returned to cook for her brother.
Three husbands had now died on her,
Leaving her lonely, seeking more,
Still young and the niece of Arthur.
Arthur's reign was a golden one,
Then came the summer without sun,
Year five hundred and thirty-six.
Once again I rode with Arthur,
Loyally south of our border,
Twrch Trwyth's invasion to fix.
In Cwm Cerwyn we boldly fought,
Where brave Guydre death's ticket bought,
Leaving Arthur without an heir.

Gwynlliw was wooing Gwenhwyfar,
Cadwg was offending Arthur,
Neighbours in dispute arms did bear.
Cadwg had fasted against us,
We chose his side beside the Wysg
When red and white cows turned to fern.
That brat Medrawt struck Gwenhwyfar,
'Holy' Illtyd made Arthur fear
Maelgwn – against Gwynedd to turn.

At this time from Deganwy came
Maelgwn's princess, Eurgain by name,
A spirited young seventeen.
Ruby and opal set in gold
Her golden hair did bind and fold,
Light blue dress worn just like a queen.
Fine woollen cloth, expensive silk,
Would she demand to bathe in milk?
With red and green bejewelled belt,
Bangle of gold, blue-sapphired wrist,
This goddess me embraced and kissed,
Both old, then young again, I felt.
Adventurous, divine dancer,
Eurgain looked to me for shelter
Far away from her father's court.

Her mother Nesta was replaced
By Sannan, from close Powys based,
As an uncle, Eurgain me thought,
One who would never betray her,
Unlike Rhun, her young half-brother,
Son of Gwalltwen, king's concubine.
With silver thread and needle skilled,
Eurgain soon planned, sewed, wove and willed
A white horse banner to be mine.

Eurgain and I the Tarrens rode,
Above Pennal, our old abode,
And the winding Afon Dyfi.
At night by full of moon I sped,
My horse not needing to be led,
To Tegfedd at Llanymawddy.
Times were hard and food very short,
Corn could not be easily bought,
But Tegfedd's cauldron always full.

Discontent spread through all the land,
Bread could not be made out of sand,
Word spread against King Arthur's rule.
Aberdyfi landed fishes,
So people could still fill dishes,
Maelgwn's Gwynedd was governed well.
'Twas June in the year of heaven
Five hundred and thirty-seven
When drums of war sounded from hell.
Brat Medrawt was implicated,
Arthur marched north discontented,
Maelgwn threatened none, called for peace.
Old man Ill-tide was the suspect,
Arthur merely Rome's toy puppet,
Used so Gwynedd's freedom might cease.
Irish in boats, men from Llydaw,
Mercenary Saxons we saw,
Join Arthur's army from the south.
Maelgwn Gwynedd called talks of peace
At the sacred summer solstice,
On sands at holy Dyfi's mouth.
Take care, said I, of treachery,
For who on Illtyd can rely?
We meet on Dyfi's southern shore,
Small party in boats, at low tide,
But Illtyd's men in bog can hide,
I sense I must prepare for war.
By Sarn Helen, Arthur's army
Could enter our territory,
Pennal would be a sitting duck.

Let's not wait to be destroyed there,
Let's entice the enemy where
We might win with a bit of luck.
Women and children all must go
To a stone circle that I know
On a ridge above Cwm Maethlon,

Along whose wooded valley side
Gwynedd's archers I now will hide,
Then we'll taunt Arthur to come on.
In the event, mid-summer's day
Nearly went old man Illtyd's way,
Fearing peace he summoned more men.
Into our boats we quickly flew,
To escape, some of them I slew
As they emerged out of the fen.
Arthur did not Sarn Helen take,
Night and next day we stayed awake,
Moving up the Dyfi valley.
'Twas my nightly route to Tegfedd,
To the niece of Arthur's warm bed,
Where road crossed river at Mawddwy.

That night twenty-one hundred men
Joined our side from Alan Fyrgan,
And in Cwm Dugoed, Saxons camped.
To such was King Arthur reduced,
Puppet of Rome, by Illtyd duped,
Foes now allies, loyal hearts damped.
Weary, before my sword I prayed
Up Cwm Cerist, where firelight made
Its glow out of King Arthur's sight.
Maelgwn me his battle plan told,
Far side of pass, reserves he'd hold,
Whilst I at ford engaged first fight.
Dawn came, rain out of grey sky broke
As forty thousand men awoke,
Horses to mount for fateful ride.
Even now, good men of peace talked
But Iddawg's deadly tongue was forked,
For his absent master Ill-tide.
Ranks of men massed on either side
Of the flowing Dyfi's divide,
As I rode to the border's ford
To say aloud, halt or we fight,
As Arthur knew was Gwynedd's right,
For Maelgwn was here his own lord.
Still, stolid, silent was the scene
Until a flash of sword was seen
Just to despatch a stray adder.
Mayhem then broke out all around
As warriors quickly swords found
And combat soon drove men madder.

Gold dragon banner I passed on,
To free hands for sword of Maelgwn,
As my nimble, grey horse I led.
Scarlet gauntlet and boots I wore,
Steely-blue mail, like fish-scales bore,
Cloak black outside but inside red.
Backwards, ever backwards I went
Up Cwm Cerist, my strength was spent,
Until the narrow pass was near.
Arthur's army was extended,
Thin, easily apprehended
By archers from trees without fear.
A perfect place for an ambush
And now Maelgwn's reserves did rush
Past me to quickly turn the tide.
To cloak of red and gold changing,
With helmet of brave wolf howling,
On the right, quickly I did ride.
Down the valley my grey horse sped,
Chasing as Arthur's army fled,
Their king struck down upon a rock.
Eda Elyn Mawr cursed be,
For Arthur's mortal blow caused he;
Tegfedd's uncle I could not mock.
Angelic Sandde led our left,
While in the centre Maelgwn cleft
With sword wielded so mightily.
Back down to the Dyfi rode we,
Victors and heroes we'd now be,
To Tegfedd I rode gratefully.

Tending wounded on the hillside
Above the battlefield I spied
My love, Tegfedd, King Arthur's niece.
Soon brought was her uncle's body
To Tydecho's chapel holy
At Mallwyd, for resting in peace.
Arthur still breathed, as I can state,
Kneeling there with Tegfedd till late,
He expired on the next morning.

Her love for me now seemed so cold,
No hero I, no victor bold,
Tegfedd's grief was overwhelming.
From Maelgwn I did learn later
How Illtyd's men came by water
When fog filled Mawddach estu'ry,
Outflanking Maelgwn's main forces,
They were chased by Sandde's horses,
By Sarn Helen for Deganwy.

Some in Ganllwyd's river were drowned,
Others on Yr Wyddfa were found
By a double of Arthur led.
Arrows were dispensed from on high,
Dealing death out of a blue sky,
And the impostor to death bled.
Meanwhile dead Arthur was taken
By Tegfedd, Gwyar and maidens
From Mawddach to Ynys Enlli.
Sick of death and bloody slaughter,
Spurned by Anna of Gwent's daughter,
A holy man I vowed to be.
Maelgwn was soon pendragon crowned
On the Dyfi estu'ry's sands
In Maeldaf's chair of waxed feathers.
Word was then brought of news for me
That Tegfedd might well pregnant be,
But her care was now her brother's.
Illtyd had claimed Arthur for Gwent,
Tegfedd and his body were sent
South to Samson on Ynys Byr.
In hot pursuit I rode down there,
Only to be left in despair
When Illtyd set the sea on fire.
When Tegfedd to Gwent then went home,
Buried Arthur, no more to roam,
I followed her most discreetly.
On mountainside above her home,
A hermit's shrine I made my own,
Near the mother of my baby.

In great secret that autumn came
Our pendragon, Maelgwn by name,
For Old Derfel to be friendly.
Reconciliation he sought,
As I to Tegfedd was brought,
Now carrying child heavily.
A good dynasty we would start,
With love restored to Tegfedd's heart,
But first one last royal request,
To carry the holy cup west
From Saxon threat, at king's behest,
Special mission by Brigit blessed.
So to Ynys Witrin we rode,
Glaston, holy Brigit's abode,
With old Blaise, Catwg and Pedrog.
Under full moon from holy spring,
Brigit a wooden box did bring,
Inside a cup whose charge I took.
Westwards we all rode into Gwent,
A rest near Cwmbran, then we went
Ceredig's Ystrad Fflur to gain.
There, at another holy well,
Fine ladies came in woods to dwell,
Amongst them Enddwyn and Eurgain.
My mission accomplished, I sped
Back to Gwent, to be with Tegfedd,
Full of life and loving intent,
But a fresh grave greeted my eyes,
A good woman told me no lies,
How Tegfedd's belly had been rent,

Illtyd's men had killed our baby,
Leaving them dead under a tree,
Telling all the Saxons to blame.
So what had Old Ill-tide to gain?
That Arthur would soon again reign?
For Tegfedd with his body came
Witness to Uncle Arthur's grave
In a riverside woodland cave,
That Illtyd now wished to deny.
My eyes blazed, with sword did I ride,
Maelgwn and Brynach at my side,
Murderer Illtyd to destroy.
In Brychan's land we dug a pit
And lit a roasting fire in it,
Above stretched Illtyd on a frame.
With a hot poker I killed him,
That evil old man, full of sin,
How would Monkish scribes clear his name?

'Tis time to close my story grim,
The next thirty years I shall trim,
My sword I did soon throw away.
To Carn Ingli, Brynach I led,
And the birds of Rhiannon fed,
Then back to Gwynedd made my way.

Keeping a lonely, wild preserve,
As Maelgwn's Myrddin I did serve,
With Eurgain as the chief priestess.
The trust of one so young and fair
Being so great, I did not dare
To risk more than an uncle's kiss.
In time, Maelgwn saw her well wed
To Elidir, prince of Rheged,
Before a plague swept o'er Gwynedd,
Year five hundred, forty-seven,
Year when Maelgwn went to heaven,
I was beside him at his death.

Great, unselfish king to the end,
Maelgwn all his subjects did send
Away from him for their safety

When sure he must infected be,
Was attended only by me,
In the chapel at Rhos-on-sea.
Maelgwn's last words I recorded,
Why had I not Eurgain married?
His son Rhun had not earned his trust,
Princess Eurgain, he did wish it,
Gwynedd's throne now to inherit.
On Ynys Seiriol I must
Lay his mortal remains to rest,
With Druid prayers he would be bless'd,
And then Maelgwn did breathe his last.
Swiftly I did as I was bade,
Sent for Elidir of Rheged,
With fair Princess Eurgain, grief-blast,
But Taliesin went around,
On Rhun's behalf making much sound
Against those by Black Moro borne.
After reaching Arfon by sea,
Eurgain witnessed great treachery,
Now Arfon's men were for Rhun sworn.
Elidir was slain close to us
On the banks of the Mewydus.
I saved Eurgain from a savage,
As spectators we had to stand
When Clydno Eiddyn burnt the land,
Causing Rhun Rheged to ravage.

76

Before the Yellow Plague he fled,
Good Bishop Deiniol had said
A living was reserved for me,
So I now retired to my llan,
Near brothers Mael and Sulien
Beside the Afon Dyfrdwy.
No flesh or fowl I ever ate,
But nuts and apples filled my plate
And I drank from my sacred spring.
Too much blood is shed on this earth,
For pow'r and riches of no worth,
All creatures, blessings let us bring.
Strange priest was I, a Myrddin still,
God and goddess, doing their will,
Riding my horse to old maids' needs,
'Til cousin Cadfan called on me
To join him on Ynys Enlli,
This Isle of Hope, our future seed,
Where male and female join as one,
And here I made the treasures come,
After Lleuddad, Abbot became,
And now from here my soul will part,
With the leaping of my old heart,
Into the arms of Rhiannon.............

The Battle of Camlan Walk 1

Distance: Four miles one way
The two ends of this linear walk may be linked by
bus no 33 (Dolgellau- Dinas Mawddwy- Machynlleth),
tel. 0870   6082608

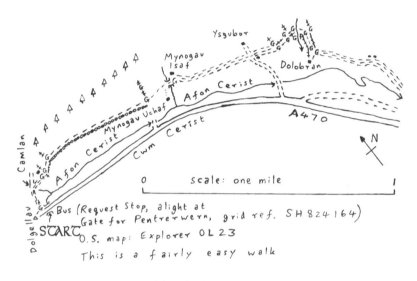

This is a fairly easy walk

KEY TO THE MAP

```
-.-,   The walking route    ....  Other path

====   Motor road           == Surfaced track

++++   Hedge or fence        ooooo  Wall

  G    Gate                  Bus  Bus stop

 ───>  Stream or river with direction of flow

 ─E→  Bridge                 •■  Buildings

 ⌀φ   Trees                 Afon is Welsh for river

  X    Campsite              ▢  Ruin
```

78

The Battle of Camlan Walk 2

Distance: Four miles one way
The two ends of this linear walk may be
linked by bus no 33 (Dolgellau- Dinas Mawddwy-
Machynlleth), tel. 0870 6082608

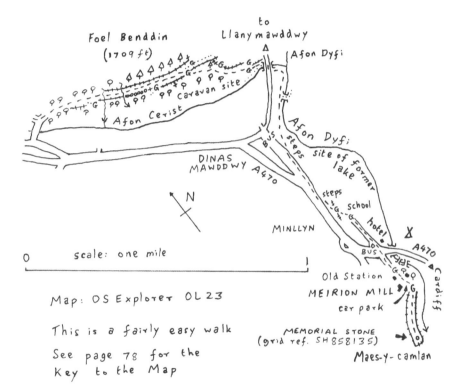

Map: OS Explorer OL 23

This is a fairly easy walk

See page 78 for the
Key to the Map

The battle started at the ford now crossed by
a seventeenth century packhorse bridge (Pont Minllyn).
Arthur's army pushed up Cwm Cerist. The tide of
battle turned at the Camlan at SH821169, then
flowed back to Maes-y-camlan (SH857132).

Admire the womb of the goddess from this walk of two miles

O.S. map:
Explorer OL 23

See page 78
for the key
to the Map

Dinas
Mawddwy

BUS

Old Station

MEIRION
MILL

car
park

START

Afon Dyfi

Coed Cefncoch

Grid ref.: SH 859 139

N

A470

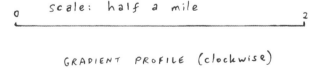

scale: half a mile

0   2

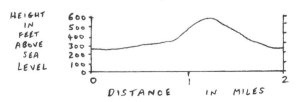

GRADIENT PROFILE (clockwise)

HEIGHT
IN
FEET
ABOVE
SEA
LEVEL

600
500
400
300
200
100
0

0   1   2

DISTANCE   IN   MILES

Visit St Tydecho's Church, Mallwyd
on a walk of over 5 miles

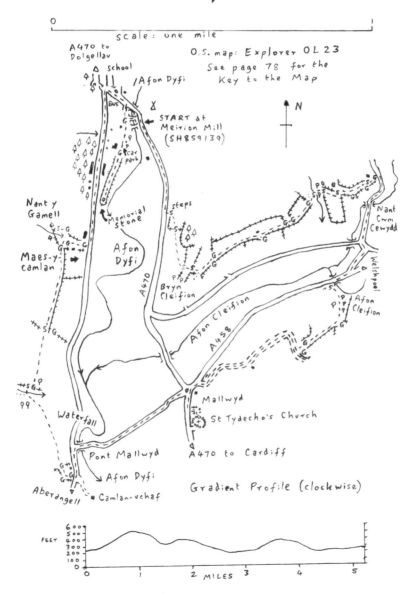

scale: one mile

A470 to Dolgellau

School

/Afon Dyfi

O.S. map: Explorer OL23
See page 78 for the
Key to the Map

↑ N

START at
Meirion Mill
(SH859139)

car park

Nant y Gamell

steps

Memorial Stone

Nant Cwm Cewydd

Maes-y-camlan

Afon Dyfi

A470

Bryn Cleifion

Afon Cleifion

Afon Cleifion

Welshpool

A458

Mallwyd

St Tydecho's Church

Waterfall

Pont Mallwyd

A470 to Cardiff

Aberangell

Afon Dyfi

Camlan-uchaf

Gradient Profile (clockwise)

FEET 600 500 400 300 200 100 0

0   1   2 MILES 3   4   5

Location Map

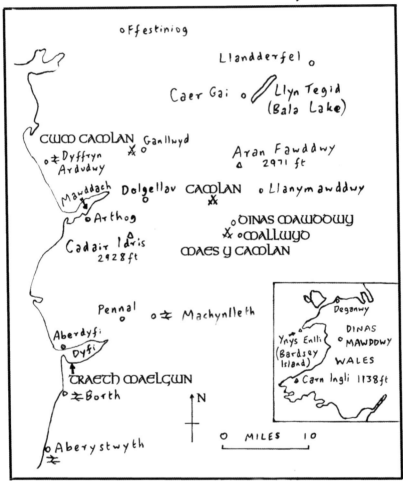

o Ffestiniog

Llandderfel o

Caer Gai o //Llyn Tegid
(Bala Lake)

CWM CAMLAN Ganllwyd
o ☡ Dyffryn ✗ o
Ardudwy

Aran Fawddwy
▵ 2971 ft

Mawddach Dolgellav CAMLAN o Llanymawddwy
o   ✗✗

o Arthog
▵
Cadair Idris
2928 ft

o DINAS MAWDDWY
✗ o MALLWYD
MAES Y CAMLAN

Pennal
o   o ☡ Machynlleth

Aberdyfi
o   Ynys Enlli
Dyfi   (Bardsey
Island)

Deganwy

DINAS
o MAWDDWY
WALES

TRAETH MAELGWN
o ☡ Borth   o Carn Ingli 1138 ft

↑ N
┼

o Aberystwyth
☡

O   MILES   1 O

☡ = RAILWAY STATION. Machynlleth is the nearest
railway station to Dinas Mawddwy. Buses run
to Dinas Mawddwy from Machynlleth and Dolgellau.

82

Others have been drawn to this place. Some can tell their own stories. These poems from Patricia John tell of the men who died here.

Untitled Poem

Since childhood I have known you,
Boy and girl companions,
Castle ramparts we explored, ditch and dyke we swam,
Then the man came forth from this tall youth's body,
Firm of flesh, kind and just, with blue sparkling eyes.
I the woman grew, still delighting in your company,
Lovers we became from childhood friends,
Then you took your leave for Camlan, yea how could I forget.
Whispered words of love among our sad farewell,
I gave you symbols of protection, ivy and sweet myrtle,
With prayers to Mother Mary for your safe return,
Did I know this was the end; my heart did,
Heavy it lay, apprehensive and cold,
No return beloved, I heard of death in battle,
Mary, where was thy protection then?
Yet later I gave thanks to thee sweet earth mother,
When from my womb came forth thy gift of life,
My love, I see you live again in different form,
Through this tall young son with blue sparkling eyes.

Last Lament

Never thought I when you journeyed o'er the land to Camlan
'Twould be our last embrace,
Death by the sword, life departed, spirit free,
Beloved, I too died in that shady grove,
My heart stopped beating at that moment as barb pierced through,
From arrow sharp and deadly true from cupid's bow,
Your voice now silent, I walk my path alone,
Yet your words of love I hear whispered on the North Wind,
Stay awhile, I am nearly through with life,
It is a shadow that lives now, await my love I cometh.

GWEDDI'R DERWYDD

RHODD, O DDUW, DY
AMDDIFFYNIAD;
AC YN AMDDIFFYNIAD, NERTH;
AC YN NERTH, DEALLTWRIAETH;
AC YN DEALLTWRIAETH,
GWYBODAETH;
AC YNG NGWYBODAETH,
CYFIAWNDER;
AC YNG NGHYFIAWNDER
EI GARIAD;
AC YN Y CARIAD YNA, CARIAD YR
HOLL FODOLAETH;
AC YN HOLL FODOLAETH,
CARIAD DUW
DUW A' I HOLL DDAIONI.

THE UNIVERSAL DRUID PRAYER

GRANT, O GOD THY PROTECTION;
AND IN PROTECTION, STRENGTH;
AND IN STRENGTH,
UNDERSTANDING;
AND IN UNDERSTANDING,
KNOWLEDGE;
AND IN KNOWLEDGE,
THE KNOWLEDGE OF JUSTICE;
AND IN THE KNOWLEDGE OF
JUSTICE, THE LOVE OF IT;
AND IN THAT LOVE,
THE LOVE OF ALL EXISTENCES;
AND IN THE LOVE OF ALL
EXISTENCES, THE LOVE OF GOD;
GOD AND ALL GOODNESS.